D0796016

THE
EVERYTHING KIDS'
SCRATCH CODING
BOOK

Dear Reader,

I have been working with coding for more than twenty-five years—from when I was just starting eighth grade in Australia. I never took a computer science class in school, so I mostly learned how to code from older kids who already knew how to code. Seeing the computer react to the code I created made me excited and motivated me to learn more. This connection to friends and a personal curiosity led me to building games from a young age, just like you!

It's my pleasure to be able to help other young coders use this tool to dream up and build their own creations. I am pleased to be part of this new wave of computer science resurgence Scratch has helped create. Remember to always be creative. Your path to being a computer scientist will go much farther when you use your inner curiosity. Picture a project that you are passionate about, start your research, make it a reality.

Have fun!

Jason Rukman

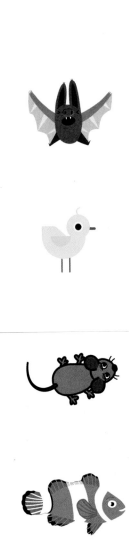

THE EVERYTHING KIDS' SCRATCH CODING BOOK

LEARN TO CODE AND CREATE YOUR OWN COOL GAMES!

JASON RUKMAN

ADAMS MEDIA

NEW YORK   LONDON   TORONTO   SYDNEY   NEW DELHI

For the powerful girls in my life,
Emma, Amelia, and Ayla,
and the ever-increasing world of technology that will shape their world.

Adams Media
An Imprint of Simon & Schuster, Inc.
57 Littlefield Street
Avon, Massachusetts 02322

An Everything® Series Book.
Everything® and everything.com® are registered
trademarks of Simon & Schuster, Inc.

First Adams Media trade paperback edition
December 2018

ADAMS MEDIA and colophon are trademarks of
Simon & Schuster.

For information about special discounts for
bulk purchases, please contact Simon & Schuster
Special Sales at 1-866-506-1949 or
business@simonandschuster.com.

The Simon & Schuster Speakers Bureau can bring
authors to your live event. For more information
or to book an event contact the Simon &
Schuster Speakers Bureau at 1-866-248-3049 or
visit our website at www.simonspeakers.com.

Interior design by Colleen Cunningham
Interior images by Kathy Konkle;
© Getty Images/Vjom, sumkinn, chuckchee,
ExpressIPhoto, Thomas Pajot
Images based upon Scratch Game Play and
used under the Creative Commons Attribution
ShareAlike 2.0 Generic License

Manufactured in the United States of America

Printed by LSC Communications, Willard,
OH, U.S.A.
10 9 8 7 6 5 4 3 2 1
November 2018

Library of Congress Cataloging-in-Publication
Data
Rukman, Jason, author.
The everything® kids' scratch coding book /
Jason Rukman.
Avon, Massachusetts: Adams Media, 2018.
Series: Everything® kids.
Audience: Ages 9-11. | Audience: Grade 4 to 6.
LCCN 2018031918 | ISBN 9781507207970 (pb) |
ISBN 9781507207987 (ebook)
Subjects: LCSH: Scratch (Computer program
language)--Juvenile literature. | Computer
games--Programming--Juvenile literature.
Classification: LCC QA76.73.S345 R83 2018 | DDC
794.8/1525--dc23
LC record available at https://lccn.loc
.gov/2018031918

ISBN 978-1-5072-0797-0
ISBN 978-1-5072-0798-7 (ebook)

Scratch is developed by the Lifelong
Kindergarten Group at the MIT Media Lab. It is
available for free at https://scratch.mit.edu.

CONTENTS

ACKNOWLEDGMENTS

Thanks to Amelia and Cheryl for all your help reviewing,
as well as trying the multitude of Scratch projects and activities.

I'd also like to thank Steven for his encouragement and passion
along with helping build fun projects and activities.

INTRODUCTION

Why have an entire book on Scratch? Well, Scratch is a great way for kids to learn computer science! It takes learning about geeky coding and makes it fun and creative. You'll learn about computers and coding while building and making your own games! Scratch coding is all about creating projects with passion and peers through play, as Mitchel Resnick, the creator of Scratch, has said in the past.

If you haven't played around with Scratch, you don't know what you're missing! Scratching results in some pretty incredible games. A lot of times, you can put just a few blocks together and get a "wow" moment where you realize you can create whatever you imagine! Scratch makes it really easy for you to learn coding with some simple tools that can do really amazing things.

Why should you learn coding? Well, first of all, it's really fun! With coding, you can make anything you want. Someone even made a version of *Minecraft* using the same Scratch coding you're going to learn about! Plus, it helps you get awesome jobs when you're older. Imagine getting paid to make your favorite video games. Someone has to do it, right? Well, a lot of those video game developers probably first got started learning about computers and coding around your age.

You'll see a lot of examples in this book. They're a great way to learn how to code. Once you understand how the example code works, you can make it your own and change it however you like. That's really important when you are learning to code. It's hard to come up with something from nothing. When you work from an example, you are starting from something that can give you some great ideas to tweak and that will help you create your own masterpiece!

This book is going to teach you exactly how to code in Scratch. It will teach you about all the different blocks and extensions, so you'll be a master in no time! Whether you're creating a Scratch project for the first time or you have played around with it before, this book is meant for you. It will teach you a whole bunch of tips and tricks that you'll need to take your project to the next level. Think of this book as a jumping-off point so you can take off and soar into the world of Scratch!

BEGIN HERE

THE BASICS OF SCRATCH

Before you learn how to code with Scratch, you need to know where it came from and what each part of Scratch is. You wouldn't be able to prepare a meal without knowing which ingredients you need! Here, you'll learn what interfaces, sprites, and blocks are and how they're used to make awesome games for you and your friends!

Scratch's Beginnings

Scratch was originally created in 2003 by Mitchel Resnick and Seymour Papert at MIT Media Lab's Lifelong Kindergarten research group. They wanted to help children of all backgrounds "to find and follow their own passions, to explore and experiment with new ideas, to develop and deliver their own voices." By 2007, their new program was ready, and Scratch 1.0 was released.

To make it easy for kids to learn, Dr. Resnick and Dr. Papert decided to make it a visual programming language (VPL). This means you write your code with blocks instead of letters and numbers. This block-coding style is a great beginner's coding language because you can experiment with the code and try different combinations with the blocks.

Since all the blocks always do exactly what they're told, it's tough to write code that doesn't work at all. But be careful! It's still very easy to create code that doesn't do what you expect it to do.

YOU WILL BE WRITING YOUR CODE WITH BLOCKS TO MAKE CODING EASY TO LEARN.

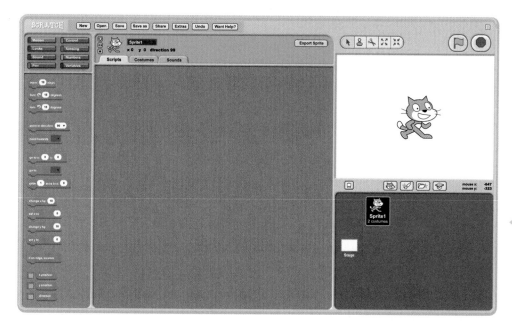

Scratch 2.0 Interface

The Different Parts of Scratch

Now that you know where Scratch comes from, let's learn about the modern version of Scratch. There are seven different elements to Scratch that you need to know to get good at coding: the interface, the sprites, the stage, the blocks, the costumes, the backdrops, and the sounds. Let's jump in!

FACT

Interface

The *interface* controls how a program looks on the screen. A program like Scratch has many coding options you can click on to do different things.

Interface

When you use a program like Scratch, what you see when you go to the website is called its *interface*. The interface for Scratch will change a little bit over time as new features are made by the Scratch team. This is what the interface for the current version of Scratch looks like. There are three main areas of the interface. The sprite area in the bottom right is for adding different characters and objects to your game. The Scratch workspace area is where you'll create your code, adjust costumes, and make any other changes in Scratch. And the stage is where you play your game! The areas won't have these borders in the actual program. This just helps highlight each separate area so you can see each one more easily. A good understanding of how these work together will help you create your projects in no time!

Scratch 3.0 Interface

Stage

Workspace Area: Code, Costumes, and Sounds

Sprite Area

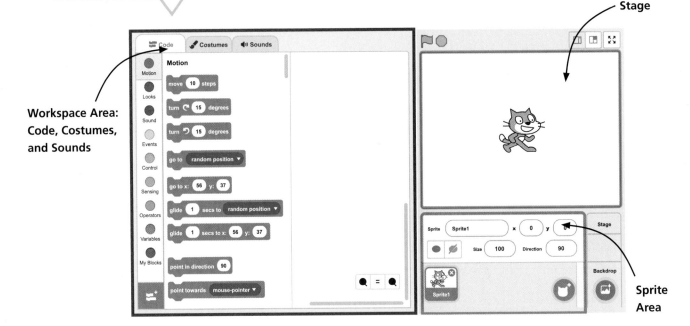

Sprites

Imagine a game without any characters or objects. That would just be a blank screen! You need something on the screen to have some fun. In Scratch you can add these different characters or objects to your projects—things like a cartoon character walking around, flying balls or meteors, and even objects in the background like a swaying tree or setting sunset. Scratch calls these characters and objects *sprites*.

Each sprite is separate from all of the other sprites and backgrounds. That means that controlling one sprite won't affect anything else on the stage. Programmers and game designers have to write their code this way or else a sprite could leave little pieces of itself behind when it touches another sprite.

Scratch doesn't stop you from making as many sprites as you want, but be careful. While more sprites seem like they would be more fun, having too many can make it hard to play your game. When you move a few sprites around on the screen, everything will work smoothly on almost any computer. But if you have a lot of sprites going at once, it can be hard for your computer to keep track of everything and it will slow everything down. No one wants a glitchy game, so make sure you're not using too many sprites, usually no more than ten to twenty.

I'M A SPRITE!

FACT

Sprites first came into existence in 1979 with the game *Galaxian* by Namco.

QUESTION

I still can't see my sprite on the stage. Where is it?

Try selecting your sprite and making it visible by clicking the *eye* button. If you still can't see it, make sure x and y are both 0. That will put it in the center of the stage. Finally, make sure its size is 100 so it's not too small to see.

▶ SPRITE AREA

The sprite area is where you can see and change all of the different sprites you're using in your project.

See the different boxes at the top of the sprite area? Here you can change things like the sprite's name, size, and location (using the x and y boxes—you'll learn more about what these mean in Chapter 2), as well as whether you can see the sprite or not and which way it is facing.

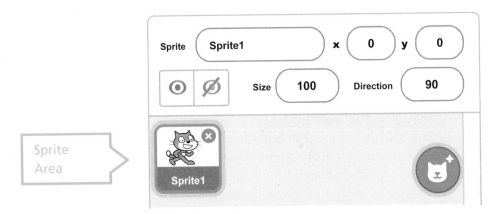

The sprite area is also where you add sprites to your project. There are four ways to add a new sprite: you can choose one, you can paint one of your own, you can use a random sprite, or you can load a picture you have saved on your computer.

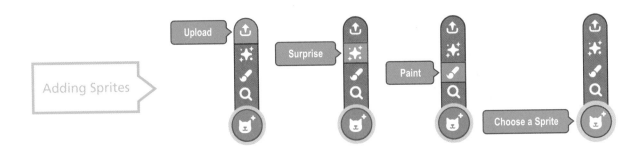

You can even add text as a sprite! Make sure you change the font size instead of trying to expand or shrink the text. That will make sure the text is easy to read and not fuzzy.

▶ BITMAPS AND VECTORS

Now that you know how to get your sprites, you need to know about the two different types of sprites: *bitmaps* and *vectors*. Bitmap sprites are drawn with *pixels*, which are tiny, tiny dots on the screen. Everything that you see on the screen is made up of pixels. You can see this if you zoom in really closely to a bitmap sprite.

ESSENTIAL

When the computer saves a picture by pixels, it is creating a bitmap image by remembering every tiny dot (known as a *pixel*) that it is made of.

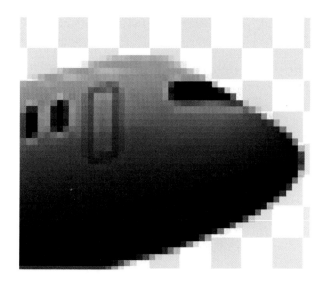

Bitmap Sprite

The other type of sprite is a vector sprite. To draw a vector sprite, the computer doesn't remember every pixel like in a bitmap. It instead remembers the different lines and shapes that are drawn! For example, when you draw a bitmap line, the computer remembers that as a long string of pixels. A vector line would be remembered simply as a line. For more complex shapes, vector sprites remember more spots along a path to draw any curved lines. This helps the edges of vector sprites stay smooth when you zoom in, unlike with bitmap sprites.

FACT

Vector Image

When the computer saves a picture by how it was drawn (by remembering each part that was drawn separately, such as a circle or line, instead of the separate dots or pixels that it is made of), it is creating a vector image.

Vector Sprite

When you go to draw or edit a sprite in the *Costumes* tab, you'll see a big blue button that says either *Convert to Bitmap* or *Convert to Vector* so you can choose what type of sprite you want. Be careful though! When you switch your sprite from a vector to a bitmap, the computer will forget how everything was originally drawn and the sprite won't come back if you switch back to vector mode.

There are a few differences between bitmap sprites and vector sprites that will help you decide which one you should use. Bitmap sprites usually have better color and shading since each pixel can be just the right color it needs to be. But they can be a little more difficult to change once you've drawn them. If you might need to edit the sprite after you've drawn it, it's better to use a vector sprite, which makes changing things really easy. Usually photos or pictures are bitmaps, and hand-drawn cartoonlike characters are vectors.

FACT

Pixel

Pixels are the dots your computer can draw to the screen. The number of pixels on your computer screen is called your *resolution*.

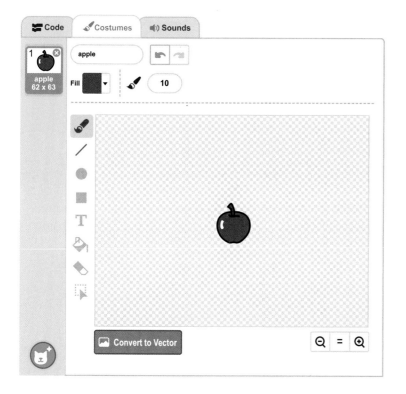

Costumes Tab

USUALLY PHOTOS OR PICTURES ARE BITMAPS, AND HAND-DRAWN CARTOONLIKE CHARACTERS ARE VECTORS.

The Stage

The stage is where your finished project is shown. The stage can have different backdrops and all of the sprites you add. If you add more than one backdrop, you can choose to switch between them using code blocks. You will learn more about that in Chapter 3. Using a backdrop can be a nice way to add some style to your project without getting in the way of your sprites.

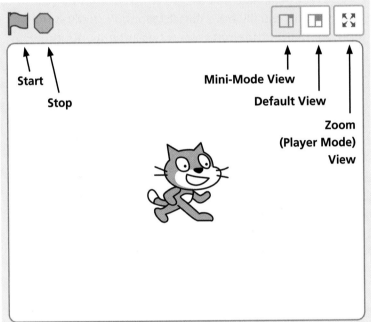

You'll also see a green flag and a red stop sign in the upper left corner of the stage. You can start or stop your project using these simple icons.

The stage also has three buttons in the top right corner.

- The first button puts the stage into mini-mode. If you have a lot of blocks and you want to see more of them at once, you can use this button to make more room.
- The second button is the default view of the stage. It should be what you see when you first start a new project.
- The last button is the *zoom* (also known as the *player mode*) button. It doesn't quite expand to full-screen mode, just to the full size of the window that Scratch is in. It hides the other areas of Scratch, so you won't see the workspace or sprite areas. This is useful when you just want to play the project.

Blocks

Just adding sprites onto the stage doesn't seem very fun. You need them to do something! You tell your sprites what to do by combining blocks together. This is known as the *script* or *code*.

Each block has a different type and color that always match. For example, all Motion blocks are going to be blue and all of the Looks blocks are going to be purple. If you see a block in an example from this book but can't find it, go to whichever section matches the block's color and look there!

If you are looking for some more help or tutorials, click the *Tutorials* tab above the Workspace Area to get to the *How-Tos* screen. From here you can learn how to do a lot of different things, like adding a sprite or making your sprites change size.

ALERT

If your project uses the mouse a lot, you should test it in the zoom (player mode) view to make sure it works right.

FACT

Active

Active means Scratch is currently working on that set of blocks. When your script is active, you'll see a yellow glow around it.

YOU TELL
YOUR SPRITES
WHAT TO DO BY
COMBINING BLOCKS
TOGETHER.

▶ADDING BLOCKS INSIDE OTHER BLOCKS

The real power of Scratch comes from combining blocks together. Wherever you see a white oval in a block, other rounded blocks can be placed inside, and when you see a darker hexagon, a hexagon-shaped block can be put there.

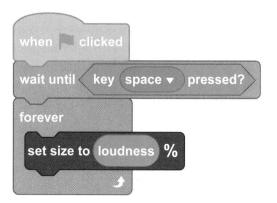

It's also possible to add circular blocks in places you might not expect. Many blocks have a drop-down menu that opens up a list of options to choose from when you click on it. For example, the "point toward _____" block, which you'll learn more about in Chapter 2, will let you choose the mouse pointer or any of the other sprites to point toward.

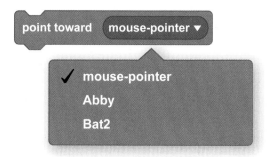

ALERT

In many cases, you can even add circular blocks to the white oval space that have different options than those listed. This isn't something you're likely to need very often, but it can be a lifesaver with some of the advanced blocks you'll see later in the book.

Not all drop-down selection blocks allow you to add another block inside for the selection. You can usually tell by looking at what shape the menu is. For example, the "when I receive _____" block has a rectangular area where you pick the option. There are no rectangle blocks in Scratch, so in this case you can't put another block inside it. You can only choose from the options already listed. After all, you can't fit a round peg into a square hole!

Other Conditional blocks allow only long hexagon-shaped blocks to be added to them, which we'll learn about in Chapter 7. An example of these blocks is the "if/then" block like this one.

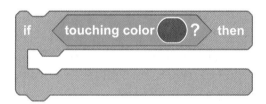

▶BACKDROPS VERSUS SPRITES

Sprites aren't the only things you can add blocks to. You can also add them to your background. However, not all of the blocks that work for sprites work for the background. This is because what you can do to a backdrop is not quite the same as what you can have a sprite do. For example, a sprite can be told to say something with a speech bubble. It wouldn't make sense for a backdrop to be told to say something. Where would the speech bubble go?

NOT ALL OF THE BLOCKS THAT WORK FOR SPRITES WORK FOR THE BACKGROUND.

▶BLOCK TYPES

Scratch groups blocks together by the type of action they create. Here are the different types of blocks and what they do.

- Motion blocks are **dark blue** and control where a sprite goes.
- Looks blocks are **purple** and can switch the backdrop or the costume for sprites. They can also make the sprite say something or even make it disappear!
- Sound blocks are a **purplish-pink** and let your project play fun noises.
- Events blocks are **yellow** and can send messages between sprites.
- Control blocks are **light orange** and control what other blocks do rather than the sprite, like make the block repeat itself or stop the script.
- Sensing blocks are **light blue** and sense things like if the sprite touches a certain color or if a key is pressed.
- Operators blocks are **green** and let you combine things together or do math.
- Variables blocks are **dark orange** and let you create special blocks that can remember a number or a word.
- My blocks are **red** and there are no presets. This is where you can make your very own blocks!

There are more blocks in the Extensions section, like Pen blocks and Music blocks, which you'll learn about later. But you probably won't use those as often as the nine types of blocks previously described.

▶BLOCK SHAPES

Hat blocks are used to start your code. Without a Hat block, any blocks you add won't do anything because nothing will tell them when to start!

YOU CAN PUT AS MANY BLOCKS AS YOU LIKE INSIDE THE C AREA.

Stack blocks can have blocks connected at the top or bottom. Use these to make your sprite do things or change in some way.

Reporter blocks are oval-shaped, and they tell you about other things in your project. For example, they can answer questions like "Where is the mouse?" or "What time is it?" These Reporter blocks have to be added to other blocks with oval cutouts to work.

Condition blocks are shaped like a hexagon. They are a special type of Reporter block that only say "yes" or "no." For example, one Condition block asks, "Is the mouse clicked right now?" Another asks, "Is 2 less than 4?" These special Reporter blocks can be added to other blocks that have hexagonal cutouts.

C blocks are for adding other blocks inside the C area. You can put as many blocks as you like inside the C area! They can make the blocks inside repeat themselves or check if other things are happening.

End blocks, or **Cap blocks**, can't have anything connected under them. They are used to stop your code.

Costumes

If the sprites always looked exactly the same, that would be pretty boring. Luckily, the creators of Scratch thought of that and gave the sprites different costumes! The costumes all look pretty close to each other, but there's a good reason for that. Many of the costumes were created so you can make it look like your sprites are moving, like in a flip-book. For example, here are the four costumes that come with the Casey sprite character.

Casey's Four Costumes

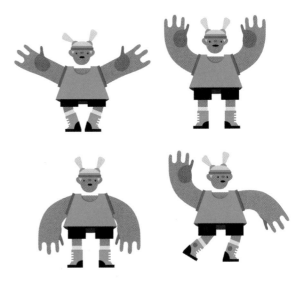

You can make it look like he's waving up and down by switching between the top two costumes, or you can make it look like he's dancing by switching between the bottom right and one of the other costumes.

You can find different costumes on the *Costumes* tab in the top left of the workspace area. If you click on *Choose a Costume*, you can choose a new costume for the sprite. You can also draw your own costumes, get a surprise costume, load other images you already have, or take a picture with a camera.

It's important to try to understand the difference between costumes and sprites. The costume is a part of the sprite, like the direction or location. You can change the costume of the sprite without deleting the previous costume. Each sprite can have a lot of different costumes, but it will show only one at a time. It's up to you to control which costume the sprite will show at any point in time.

Backdrops

Take a look at your stage right now. It's pretty lame, right? It's just the Scratch cat, not very exciting. Well, good news! You can add backdrops to make it more exciting. And you don't have to stop at just one backdrop. Your project can have multiple ones.

You add a backdrop the same way as adding a sprite and with the four same options. You can choose a backdrop the Scratch creators already made, draw one yourself, or load one from your computer. You can also choose a surprise backdrop, which will choose a random one that's already been created.

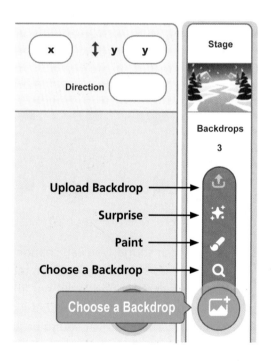

Backdrop Button Choices

ESSENTIAL

There are a number of fun ways you can use backdrops in your projects. You can switch between two different backdrops to create some really cool background effects, or you can have a different backdrop for different levels of a game!

Backdrops are not the same as sprites. You cannot move backdrops around on the screen like you can with sprites. It's possible to make it so your sprite will detect if it's touching a color that is in your backdrop, but that's not the same as detecting if two sprites are touching. For instance, you could make a maze where the maze is actually a sprite, not the background. This way, you can detect if a sprite touches the maze more easily. If your maze is a backdrop, you'd have to have your sprite detect a specific color, which won't work in some cases.

Sounds

You can make your Scratch projects a lot more fun by adding sound effects to them. Just like you can use a sprite that's already made, draw your own, or upload one, the *Sounds* section of Scratch lets you select from the hundreds of options already made, record your own sound using your microphone, choose a randomly selected sound, or upload a sound from a file.

Sound Effects Section

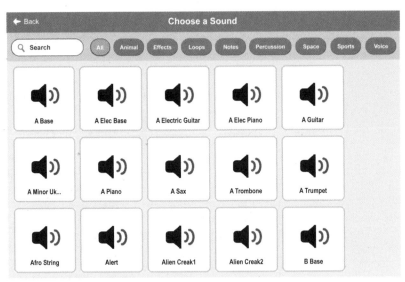

Once you've chosen your sound, you can change it to fit your project. You can make it louder or softer. You can make it go faster or slower. You can make it sound like it has an echo or play the sound backward. You can even make it sound like a robot made the noise! You can make whatever sound best fits your specific project.

Let's Get Started!

Now that you know a little bit about the different parts of Scratch, it's time to dive in and learn more about all the different programming blocks and how they can bring your project to life. Each chapter will teach you a little bit more about the different types of blocks and how you can use them to make some really fun games. Let's go!

GET A MOVE ON

MOTION

How many games do you play where you don't move at all? Not too many, right? So if you want to create something fun and enjoyable to play, you should get your sprites moving too! Some sprites can move randomly all around the screen, but most should move only in certain ways. If you're playing a game where your sprite has to jump over walls, you wouldn't use a bird. It would just fly over everything! In this chapter, you'll learn all about the sprites and the different ways you can make them move.

Setting Up Your Sprites

Everything needs a place to live. Sprites live on the stage! The stage is the space where sprites can move around. This space is two-dimensional, which means they can move only left or right and up or down. There are three things that tell a sprite where it is on the stage: the *x* variable, the *y* variable, and the direction. Before you get to make your sprites dance around the stage, you have to understand what each of these things means.

X and Y Coordinates

Each sprite has a specific *x* and *y* variable that tells you its location. A *variable* represents a number that you don't know the exact value of or might change over time. An example of this might be how many friends you have. Someone you know might have five friends while someone else might have dozens of friends. The number of friends changes depending on who you're talking about. For Scratch, the sprite's location is a variable because it can change depending on where it is on the stage.

QUESTION

What Are Coordinates?

Coordinates are two numbers, the *x* variable and the *y* variable, we use to represent a position on the stage. The first number (the *x* value) is how far to the left or right the position is from the center, which is always zero. The second number (the *y* value) is how far to the top or bottom the position is from the center.

In this example, the *x* is the orange horizontal direction and goes from –240 on the left to 240 on the right. The *y* is the blue vertical direction and ranges from –180 at the bottom to 180 at the top.

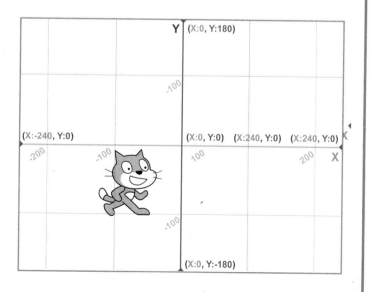

Where a sprite is on the stage from left to right, which we call the *horizontal*, is controlled by the *x* variable, and where it is from the top to the bottom, known as the *vertical*, is controlled by the *y* variable. So when a sprite moves to the left, for example, its *x* variable would change, and when it moves up, its *y* variable would change.

Which Way Did It Go?

A great way to think about direction is to picture the stage as a large piece of white paper. Lay it down flat and picture yourself standing on it. If you are told to turn clockwise (to the right) or counterclockwise (to the left), you can picture where you will now be facing. In this way, you can picture the directions for your sprites to turn as well. Just like each sprite has an *x* and *y* variable to tell you where the sprite is, it also has its own *direction* variable.

When you use a block to move a sprite, it will move in whatever direction it's currently facing. Because of this, you should understand what the numbers for the direction mean. The direction of your sprite is like a circle. When it's facing straight up, its number is 0. As the numbers get larger, the sprite spins around in the circle going clockwise until it's facing straight down. When it's facing straight down, its number is 180. If you want it to face exactly halfway between up and down, you just use the number that's halfway between 0 and 180: 90. If you want it to turn around and face to the left, you use the same numbers but make them negative. So 90 and –90 both are halfway between 0 and 180, just facing in exactly opposite directions!

If you use the "point in direction _____" block and click on the number, you get a helpful circle with an arrow to let you set which direction you want. Dragging the arrow around the circle will let you see what the numbers are for the different directions. Some of the numbers for the directions are also shown here.

These won't appear on your screen but they give you a rough idea of about where they will be. You can also set the direction value directly in the sprite area as well.

Movin' and Groovin'

Now that you know what *x* and *y* variables are, you can use them to make your sprite move! There are different ways for your sprite to move across the stage. Do you want your sprite to move immediately to the new location or watch it glide there? How you want the sprite to move will help you decide which block you should use.

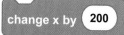

Change, Set, and Go to Location

To move a sprite immediately to a new location, you can either change or set its *x* or *y* variables using the "change x by _____" block or "set x to _____" block.

The change option will move the distance you put in while the set option will teleport the sprite to a brand-new spot. Whichever block you choose, the sprite will instantly appear in its new location.

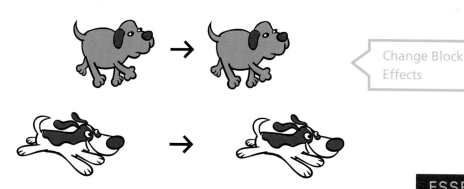

Change Block Effects

Take a look at the dogs. The first dog was told to "change x by 200," and the second dog was told to "set x to 200." Our second dog teleports (meaning it disappears and instantly reappears somewhere else) much farther across the screen to where its *x* value will be 200 (remember *x* can be any number between –240 to the left and 240 to the right). The first dog teleports by a distance of 200 instead.

ESSENTIAL

Think of "change x by _____" as being the same as "move _____ steps" and "set x to _____" as meaning "go to _____."

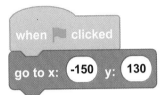

Just like "set x to _____" will move the sprite to a specific spot horizontally and "change x by _____" will move it horizontally for a specific distance, "set y to _____" will move a sprite to a specific spot vertically and "change y by _____" will move it vertically by that number of steps. There's even a block that will set both *x* and *y* at the same time! "Go to x: _____ y: _____" is the perfect shortcut to using both "set x to _____" and "set y to _____" in one step.

"Go to _____" is another shortcut block that you can use to move a sprite to new locations. It has several options. The first option is "random position." This will move the sprite somewhere else on the stage. The second option is "mouse-pointer." This moves the sprite wherever the mouse is when this block is run. When you want someone playing your project to use the mouse to point to click on some of your sprites on the stage, you can make a sprite a crosshair and have it follow wherever the mouse is. There are also options for each of the other sprites you have on the stage. These will move your current sprite to the selected sprite when the block runs.

Gliding

The sprites don't have to just teleport from one spot to the next. You can watch them move too! Use the "glide _____ secs to x: _____ y: _____" block to make your sprite move from one spot to another in a certain number of seconds. The sprite will end up in the same spot as if you used "go to x: _____ y: _____," but it shows the sprite moving to the new location and lets you control how much time it takes to get there.

ESSENTIAL

"Go to _____" is a great option when you have an enemy or monster that you want to teleport around on the stage.

ALERT

Repeating the "move _____ steps" block ends up looking exactly like "glide _____ secs to x: _____ y: _____," but the animation might not be as smooth as you want. You should use the glide feature when you want a smooth timed animation.

Gliding

Time to Go Home

Have you ever heard the phrase, "There's no place like home"? Well, this is also true for Scratch! Every time a project starts, sprites should start from their home too. That way your sprites will behave the same every time you run your project, with sprites always starting at the same spot and facing in the same direction. It's often best to set your sprite's location and direction right after your Hat block.

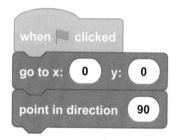

Move the Sprite

The "move _____ steps" block lets the sprite walk in whatever direction it's facing. If your sprite is facing to the right and moves ten steps, its x coordinate will go up by ten. If the sprite's facing straight up and it moves ten steps, its y coordinate will go up by ten.

Moving with Direction

Up until now the blocks for movement have just been moving the sprite in whatever direction it was facing. Since direction is also a variable, you can change the direction a sprite is facing before telling it to move.

Set Sprite Direction

If you know exactly which direction you want your sprite to go, use the "point in direction _____" block. As you saw previously, this block uses numbers to change the direction of the sprite, anywhere from –180 to 180.

YOU CAN CHANGE THE DIRECTION A SPRITE IS FACING BEFORE TELLING IT TO MOVE.

Other times you may want to change the direction of your sprite only a little bit. The "turn ↻ _____ degrees" and "turn ↺ _____ degrees" blocks change the direction of the sprite in either a clockwise or counterclockwise direction. For example, you might use these blocks for steering a car to the left or right when someone playing your game presses the *left* or *right arrow* keys.

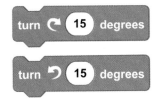

The last block for changing the direction of your sprite is the "point toward _____" block. This immediately changes the direction of the sprite toward something else on the stage. There is always at least one choice for this block. "Mouse-pointer" will point your sprite toward the location of the mouse while the code is running. You might use this to have a sprite follow the mouse around on the stage.

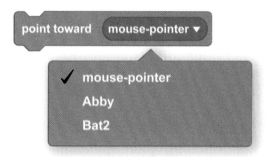

Set Rotation Style

Sometimes you might want your sprite to move around the screen in different directions, but you don't want it to face that way. For example, you might want it to be looking to the left but move up. You can do this by changing its rotation style. You set the rotation style for each sprite with the "set rotation style _____" block.

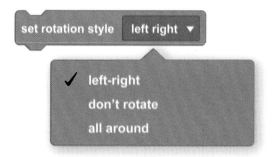

Setting "set rotation style <u>all around</u>" tells the sprite it can freely face in whichever direction you tell it. Take a look at the next example using the "<u>all around</u>" rotation style. You can see that each time the sprite moves, it faces a new direction.

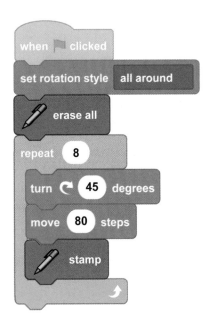

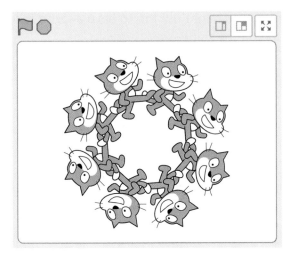

If you set the rotation style to "<u>left-right</u>," the sprite can face only left or right. In this case, when a sprite's direction is even slightly toward the left or the right, it will also face completely to the left (–90°) or right (90°). If you look at the following example, you'll notice that the script is exactly the same as the previous one except the rotation style is changed. See how the sprite faces only to the left or right instead of in whichever direction like in the previous example?

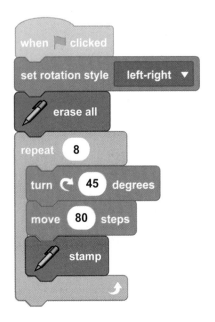

"Don't rotate," the last setting, stops a sprite from turning at all! It doesn't matter what the direction is set to, the sprite will always face to the right.

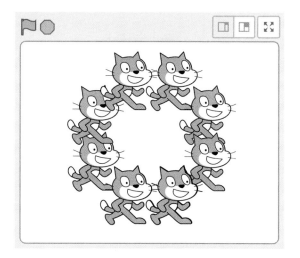

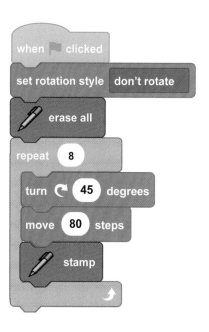

In all these examples though, you can see the sprite moves to exactly the same location each time. When a sprite moves in its current direction with a "move _____ steps" block, it will still move in the direction set, regardless of its rotation style.

Bounce Around

The "move _____ steps" block is great, but what happens when you get to the edge of the stage? By itself, it will just get stuck at the edge of the stage! That's why you need the "if on edge, bounce" block. If one of the blocks makes your sprite touch the wall and your next block is "if on edge, bounce," it will make your sprite change directions as if it has bounced off that edge.

if on edge, bounce

QUESTION

Why doesn't my sprite point in the direction I set? Why does it go upside down sometimes?

If your sprite is upside down, you might have the rotation style set to "all-around" when you want it to be "left-right." Setting it to "left-right" will make sure the sprite stays upright and just turns the other way while "all-around" will make the sprite spin in circles.

Motion Variables

If you look at the bottom of the set of motion blocks, you'll see three oval-shaped blocks. These are the sprite's *motion variables*.

Each of these has a checkbox next to it to display its value on the stage.

There are times when you will need to use these variables in your blocks of code. For example, perhaps you have a game that has a ball bouncing off a paddle at the bottom of the screen. To see if the player has missed the ball, you might check if the "y position" variable for the ball is less than the "y position" variable for the top of the paddle. You'll have to use more advanced blocks for something like this, but you'll learn about those a little later in the book.

Now that you know all about how to get your sprites moving, let's use it to have some fun! For this activity, you are going to visit some characters in the ocean.

ALERT

The bottom of the screen is −180, so if you check if the "y position" is less than, say −160, it will usually work to detect that the player has missed the ball.

Activity | Visiting Friends

EASY

1. Choose a Fun Backdrop

Let's start a new project. In this example you don't need Scratch Cat (added automatically), so go ahead and click the little *x* in the sprite area to remove it.

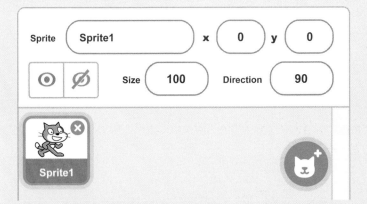

Sprite Deletion

Remember when we showed how to choose a backdrop? Pick a backdrop for your project now. For the ocean visit, you might choose one like this one.

Underwater Backdrop

2. Set Things Up

Any good Scratch project needs some sprites, right? Add in a main sprite that will move around the screen and a few others for the main sprite to visit on his or her trip around the ocean.

Added Sprites

Drag each of the sprites where you want them to be for their starting positions. Some of your sprites might be facing the wrong direction or be too big or too small. You can adjust them by setting their size and direction in the sprite area. For example, the shark in this example has been set to 50 percent of its normal size and has its direction set to –90, or pointing to the left.

ESSENTIAL

Did you notice that the "go to x: _____ y: _____" block was already filled in with some numbers for the *x* and *y*? It always uses the numbers of where the sprite is when you first grab the "go to x: _____ y: _____" block. This is a great way to save time to move sprites around to specific locations.

go to x: 200 y: -91

Sprite Area

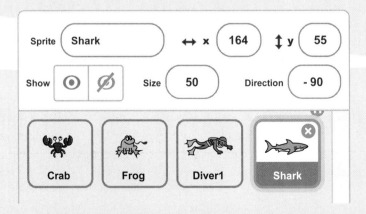

To avoid having your sprites go upside down though, you'll also need to set the rotation style to "left-right." Remember how to do that? The diver is going to move around for this project, so you need to first add a block of code to tell him where you want him to start from each time. Drag out the "when green flag clicked" from the Events blocks section and then grab a "go to x: _____ y: _____" block and connect them together.

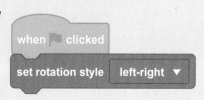

3. Visit Friends

This is a fun picture, but we want to get our main sprite moving around more and visiting his friends. To do that, drag your main sprite (in this example, it's the diver) to the next location you want him to move to and then grab a "glide _____ secs to x: _____ y: _____" block. It will be set to the coordinates for the new location automatically for you. In this example, it also changes the glide time to two seconds so the diver doesn't move too quickly.

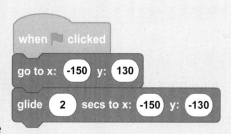

Repositioned Sprite

Now have your main sprite say "hi" to his first visitor. You'll get to explore the Looks blocks more in the next chapter, but you can use the "say _____ for _____ seconds" block here to make this project more fun.

Now move on to visiting the next friend. You have to first move the diver up above the frog so he doesn't just swim right through it to get to the crab. Moving the diver above the frog and adding the next "glide" block will look like this.

Sprite
Moving Up

```
when [flag] clicked

go to x: -150 y: 130

glide 2 secs to x: -150 y: -130

say Hi, Froggy! for 2 seconds

glide 1 secs to x: -91 y: -81
```

Then move the diver across to visit the crab by dragging out another "glide" block and "say" block. It will look like this.

Sprite Gliding and Speaking

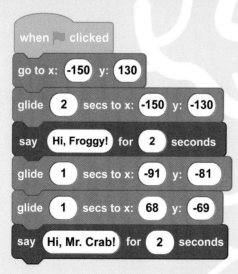

For the final steps the diver is going to visit the shark, but he gets scared when he sees him! He'll want to swim away to a random location anywhere on the stage, hopefully away from the shark!

Final Steps

ALERT

Now you can go ahead and create your own story. If you pick a space backdrop, you might like to have your main sprite visit some scary aliens, or maybe you want your main sprite to visit some animals at the zoo. Use your imagination and have fun!

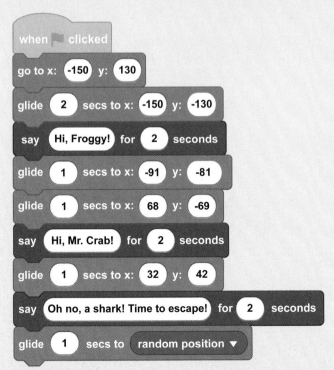

LOOKING GOOD

LOOKS AND ANIMATION

Think about what you look like. Do you always look exactly the same every single day? No, you wear different clothes every day and get different haircuts and things like that. In Scratch you can make changes to how things look as well. The Looks blocks allow you to change backdrops, costumes, colors, what sprites are saying, and more. If you want to get your sprite looking great, you'll want to find out how to give it just the right touch-ups. Let's learn about some of the different blocks that can change what your game looks like.

Costumes

You learned a little bit about costumes back in Chapter 1 and how to change them using the *Costumes* tab. Now we're going to learn how to use the blocks to change costumes while the script is running.

Each sprite has one or more costumes. Each costume is a different image. If you click on a sprite and then click on the *Costumes* tab near the top of the screen, you will see all of the costumes for that sprite.

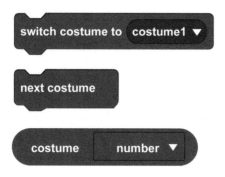

> **FACT**
>
> **Costume**
>
> The *costume* is the picture or image that a sprite displays with. Set a sprite to a specific costume to have it display that image on the stage.

Costumes Tab

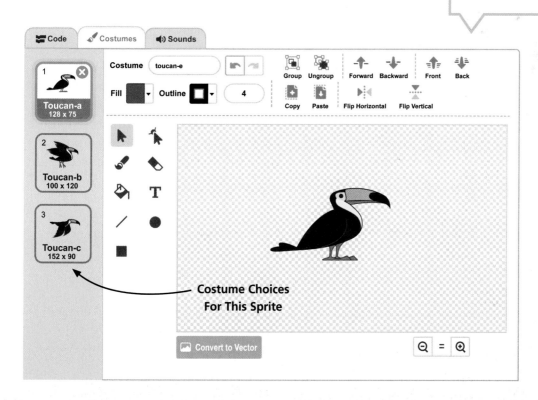

Costume Choices
For This Sprite

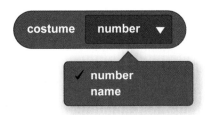

Each costume has a number and a name. These are two of a sprite's Looks variables. Each sprite has its own separate costume number and name variables since each sprite might have a different costume.

You might be wondering when you would use these variables. Good question. Here's an example. Does your sprite have special powers in your game? Perhaps it can power up and get stronger with a different costume. You can have the game check the costume name or number to see if it can defeat certain enemies.

You can click on the first, second, or third costume here to change which costume the toucan will show on the stage. But what if you want to change the costume in the middle of a game? You can't have the player stop the game, choose a different costume, then start the game again!

One way you can change the costume using blocks is with the "switch costume to _____" block. This lets you switch the costume to whichever one you want. You can go from the second costume to the third costume and back again (skipping the first one) so it looks like the toucan is flying! If you don't want the costumes to switch in a specific order, you can use the "next costume" block. This will simply change the costume to the next one in line instead of going to one you choose.

EACH COSTUME HAS
A NUMBER AND
A NAME.

Backdrops

Just like with your sprites' costumes, you can have quite a few backdrops too! You even can change them the same way you change your sprites' costumes. If you go to the *Costumes* tab after clicking on the stage workspace, you'll see all of the backdrops you've chosen for your project so far and can switch which one you want. And just like you can switch your sprites' costumes with the "switch costume to _____" or "next costume" blocks, you can choose your backdrop with the "switch backdrop to _____" block or switch to the next one with the "next backdrop" block. You can also use the "switch backdrop to _____" block to go back to the last backdrop or use a random backdrop.

switch backdrop to backdrop1 ▼

next backdrop

There is one more block that switches the backdrop that's a little different from the rest: the "switch backdrop to _____ and wait" block. This block works with a block in the yellow Events blocks section called "when backdrop switches to _____." The "switch backdrop to _____ and wait" block will change the backdrop and then wait for all of the codes that start with the "when backdrop switches to _____" block before it moves on to the next block. You'll learn more about what "wait" means in Scratch in Chapter 5.

switch backdrop to backdrop 1 ▼ and wait

✓ backdrop1
next backdrop
previous backdrop
random backdrop

There's one Looks variable you can use with backdrops: the "backdrop _____" block. Just like the "costumes _____" block, there are two options you can choose: number or name. When you click on this block, it will tell you either how many backdrops you have chosen (number) or what the name of the backdrop you've chosen is (name).

backdrop   number ▼

✓ number
name

Take a look at this picture. If I used the "backdrop <u>number</u>" block, what would come up? What about if I changed it to "backdrop <u>name</u>" instead? If you said "two" for the first question and "Party" for the second, you're right!

1

Jurassic
676 x 391

2

Party
505 x 382

Size

All of the sprites you can choose from Scratch are usually about the same size. But that doesn't make sense, does it? An elephant and a doughnut aren't the same size! Their sprites shouldn't be either!

Well luckily, you can change the size of your sprites with both the "change size by _____" block and the "set size to _____ %" block. Just like the "change" and "set" blocks you saw in Chapter 2, these blocks either make the sprite grow by the number you put in the white oval or set the size to that number.

Be careful though. You can make a sprite only so large or small. You can't make the sprite's size zero or it will disappear! And you can't make the sprite's size too big or you won't even be able to tell what it is! How large can you go? Once the size of the sprite is about twice the size of the stage, you can't make it any bigger. Can you work out what size that would be? Usually it's several thousand percent for most sprites. Don't worry though. Setting it to the max still makes the sprite look *ginormous*! If you want to get the sprite back to its normal size, change the size to 100 (100 percent). That's considered the normal size for every sprite.

Every sprite remembers its current size, and the last size of each sprite is also saved with your project. This means when you come back to work on it next time, each sprite will still be the same size. You can tell what size it is by looking at the sprite area and checking the number in the Size field. You can also show the size of the sprite in the top left corner of the stage by checking the box next to the "size" Looks variable.

Show and Hide

Sometimes you don't want a sprite to appear right away in your game. That's what the "show" and "hide" blocks are for! They will make a sprite appear or disappear!

Control when your sprites show up with these blocks. Maybe you don't want a character in your game anymore, but it might come back. Maybe there's an obstacle that your character needs to get by and once you get past it, it should disappear.

The "show" and "hide" blocks are great for that! Be careful though. Any other effects that you have going on with the sprite also disappear when you hide it. For example, if a sprite tries to say something, it will immediately disappear once it is hidden.

Sometimes you might have a sprite that doesn't need to show up right away when your project starts. You can hide these sprites right after the green flag is clicked and show them when you want them to appear.

Say and Think

Even if you can see your sprite, it still can't talk directly to you. But it can still say and think things! This is great for leaving messages to other kids playing your game or just to make your game a little more fun!

There are two different kinds of blocks that you can use: the "say _____" block or the "think _____" block. These blocks keep your speech or thought bubble up until another "say _____" or "think _____" block is played. This lets you make your sprite say or think different things as the game goes along!

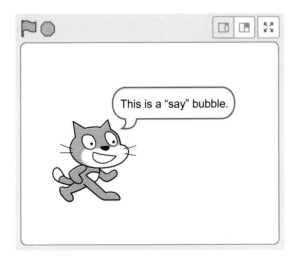

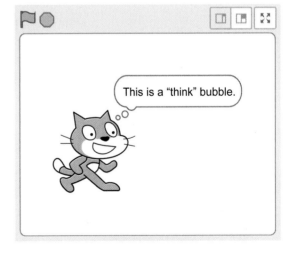

If you want your speech or thought bubble to go away after a certain amount of time, you can use the "say _____ for _____ seconds" or "think _____ for _____ seconds" blocks. This means the blocks won't move on to any following blocks until that amount of time has passed. Your bubble will show up for exactly that amount of time, and then it will go away.

say Hello! for 2 seconds

think Hmm... for 2 seconds

A neat trick is to have your sprite speech bubble show up but to hide your sprite. Set its "ghost effect" to 100. You'll learn more about this effect (and others!) a little later in the chapter. You might like to do this if you don't want your character visible anymore but still want it to say something.

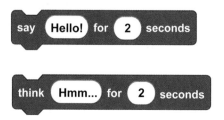

Create Some New Looks

What if you've looked at all of the costumes for a sprite and you're still not happy with how it looks? Well, Scratch has a solution for you! You can use graphic effects to make your sprite look even more different!

There are a whole bunch of really cool effects that you can put on your sprite. You do this with the "change _____ effect by _____" and "set _____ effect to _____" blocks. If you want to get rid of all of the changes you've made, use the "clear graphic effects" block.

FACT

Graphic Effects

Graphic effects change how the entire sprite looks, even if you change its costume.

ALERT

If your script changes a sprite's graphic effects, it's good practice to clear your graphic effects at the very start after a "green flag" block. This sets everything back to normal so your game always looks the same when it starts.

Let's take a look at all of the effects you can create with these blocks.

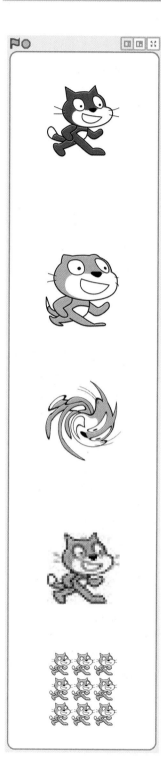

Color

The first effect you can play with is changing the color of your sprite! You can change it to be pink or green or blue or purple or any color in between using this effect. If you want the color to change a lot, like going from yellow to dark blue, you should set the number in the block to be really high, up to 200. If you want it to only change a really tiny amount, like going from a light blue to a dark blue, use a really low number. Let's take a look at Scratch Cat with its "color effect" set to 100.

Fisheye

This effect makes the middle of a sprite look really big and the outer part of the sprite look really small. The larger the number of the effect, the more of a "bubble" effect you'll see from the sprite. Here's what Scratch Cat looks like with the "fisheye effect" at 150.

Whirl

This effect makes it look like your sprite is all twisted up! It twists your sprite around a center point to make it look like it's spinning around. This is what Scratch Cat looks like with the "whirl effect" set at 200, but you can use numbers much higher for even more whirl effect.

Pixelate

Pixelating your sprite makes it look fuzzier, like a 1980s video game. You can use this one if you don't want people playing the game to know which sprite you're using. Here's the "pixelate effect" on Scratch Cat set to 20. Higher numbers will make it even fuzzier and harder to know who it is.

Mosaic

This effect lets you create many smaller copies of your sprite in the same space. Set the number higher for more copies to appear! Here's what happens when you set the "mosaic effect" to 9.

Brightness

Just like you change the brightness on your phone screen, you can also change the brightness of your sprite. The more you raise the brightness, the lighter and lighter it will get until everything is bright white! Let's see what Scratch Cat looks like with a "brightness effect" of 50.

Ghost

This effect makes your sprite more transparent, which means you can see through it more easily, like a ghost! The higher the number you use, the easier it is to see through it, though it will still have the same colors. This is what a "ghost effect" of 50 looks like on Scratch Cat.

Combining Effects

You don't have to have just one effect going at a time. You can use a couple of these blocks in a row to create some really cool effects. For example, if you want four blue Scratch Cats in a square to look fuzzy, you could use the "color effect" combined with the "mosaic effect" and the "pixelate effect."

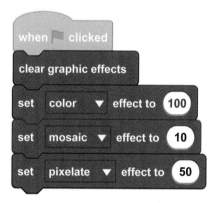

ESSENTIAL

The "ghost effect" can also be used to "hide" your sprite without using the "hide" block. Why would you want to do this? Well, it can be useful if you want the "say" or "think" bubbles to show up but not your sprite. They won't show if your sprite is hidden, but they will show if your sprite's "ghost effect" is set to 100 (which makes it invisible).

Animating Effects

By changing an effect rapidly, you can create animation-style effects. You can create an animated effect by repeating the "change _____ effect by _____" block. In the following example, if you hold down the space bar, it will change the sprite's "pixelate effect" together with a "ghost effect." This results in a slow pixelation and fade out of the sprite (see some of the different frames in the following diagram of what happens over time). Then you can click the green flag to reset it back to normal.

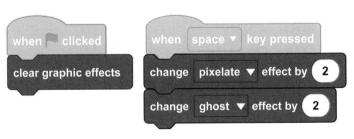

The blocks here animate the sprite to change its effect to "pixelate" combined with a disappearing effect using "ghost."

Layers

Sometimes you might be looking for your sprite and not be able to find it. It might be hiding behind something else! You can bring it in front of everything else with the "go to _____ layer" block. That lets it cut in front of all the other sprites on the screen so you can be sure to see it.

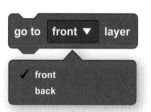

If you want a sprite in front of some sprites but behind others, you can use the "go _____ _____ layers" block. This lets you move a sprite behind or in front of other sprites without sending it all the way to the front or back. Think of this like cutting in front of your friend in line for lunch. You would be going forward one layer in the line, and your friend would be going back one layer.

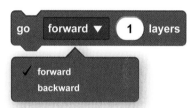

Let's do an example with the Lion, Beachball, and Crab sprites. Can you tell which sprite is in the front layer and which is in the back?

If you said the Lion is in the front layer and the Crab is in the back, you're right!

Now if you tell the Beachball sprite to "go to <u>front</u> layer," it will move the ball up. If you tell the Beachball sprite to "go <u>backward</u> <u>1</u> layer," it will move the ball down. This is really useful if you want to hide a sprite behind another one.

Activity | Tell a Story!

EASY

In this activity, you are going to tell a story of two characters getting ready for a birthday party.

1. Choose Your Sprites

Add two sprites to the stage. You can pick any sprites you like, but consider choosing ones that have more than one costume. This example uses the cat and monkey sprites.

2. Create Your Scene

Select a backdrop for the party scene. You can select an existing backdrop from the library, or you can upload your own picture. This example uses the Witch House as the party scene.

ALERT

You can see if a sprite has multiple costumes when you move your mouse over a sprite you are selecting. It will run through the different costumes it has if there are more than one.

Witch House Backdrop

3. Start the Conversation

Have your characters plan how to decorate for the party. For example, you could have the cat say, "How about we add some balloons?" Then the monkey can reply, "That's a great idea!"

You don't want them talking at the same time though. We're going to use an Events block that you haven't seen before called the "wait _____ seconds" block. As you would imagine, this block waits for a certain amount of time before the next block runs. Add that in before the monkey's "say _____ for _____ seconds" block so it doesn't talk at the same time as the cat. Since the cat's dialogue is shown for two seconds in this example, the monkey should wait two seconds before showing its dialogue.

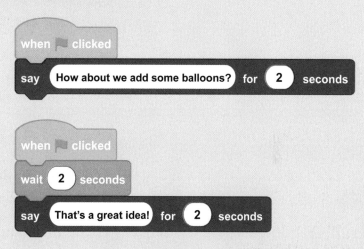

4. Add Balloons

If you want your monkey and cat to have some balloons at their party, you will have to add some blocks to show them after they have finished talking. Let's add a balloon sprite. But that seems a little too big, and you don't want it to show up at the start. What blocks do you think you should use?

You always want the balloon to start with its first costume so add a "switch costume to _____" block. You are going to add more balloons, so you'll be changing the other balloons to a different costume.

The balloons should show up after the monkey finishes talking. That means you need to add a "wait _____ seconds" after the "switch costume to _____" block. How much time do you think you should set it for? Well, the cat spoke for two seconds and then the monkey spoke for two seconds, so the balloons should show up after four seconds.

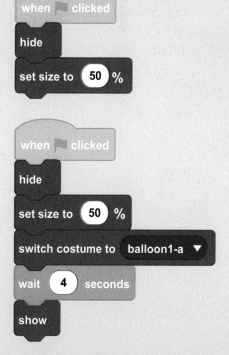

A party with just one balloon is no fun. Let's get some more! Right-click on the balloon sprite and select "duplicate" twice. You should now have three balloons. Drag them around on the stage where you want them to be, then click on each balloon in the sprite area and change the blocks of code to have a different costume. This way each balloon will look different.

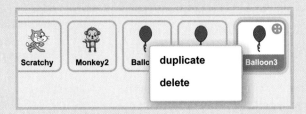

5. Blow Up the Balloons

In this example, the balloon size is set to 50 percent of its original size. Let's blow up the balloons to make them bigger! First, the cat and monkey should talk about it though. Let's add a few more "say _____ for _____ seconds" blocks to Scratch.

Now we have to make the balloons blow up. First, you want to wait for the cat and the monkey to get finished talking, so you should probably add another "wait _____ seconds" block, this time for five seconds. Then add a few "change size by _____" blocks with "wait _____ seconds" in between to watch the balloons get bigger and Bigger and BIGGER!

6. Now It's Time to Dance!

Now that the party is decorated, it's time to have some fun! Let's have the cat and monkey do a few dance moves by changing their costumes back and forth. And there you go! You just created a nice little dance party with the cat and the monkey.

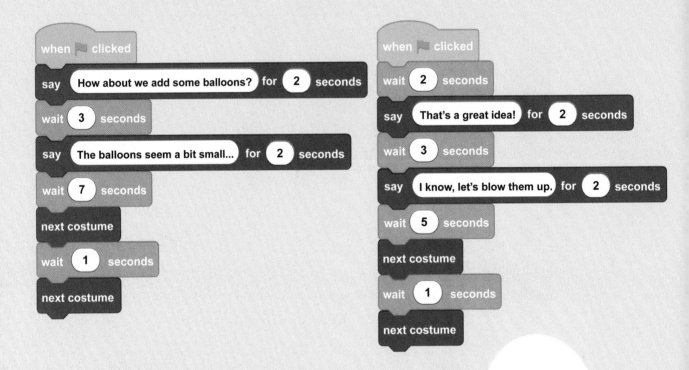

Now that you have all the blocks you need, click the green flag and see all your characters in action!

SOUNDS GOOD TO ME

SOUNDS

Think about your favorite games, movies, and TV shows. Are they silent? No! They have people talking and music playing and noise all around! Well, you can add sounds to your game too!

Sound Workspace

The sound workspace is found by clicking on the *Sounds* tab in the top left corner of the screen. This is where you see all of the sounds of either the current sprite you have selected or the stage and where you can add, delete, or change any of them. You'll also find a pink box where you can "see" the sound. The farther apart the top wavy line is from the bottom wavy line, the louder the sound will be when you hear it.

Sounds Tab

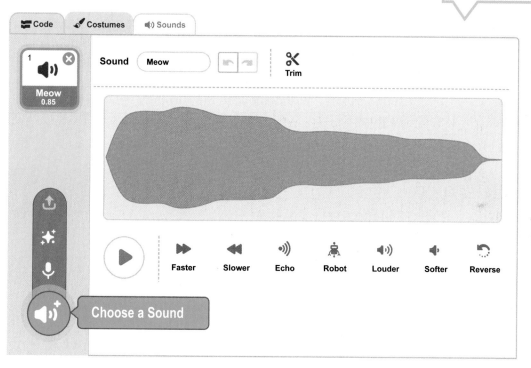

Many sprites already come with their own sounds. For example, the Cake sprite comes with a birthday sound, and Scratch Cat comes with a meow sound. The stage comes with a default pop sound.

ESSENTIAL

Each sprite and stage has its own separate set of sounds, so as you select each one, you may notice the list of available sounds change.

If you're using a sprite that doesn't come with its own sound, don't forget that you can add any sound you want by clicking on the *Sounds* tab in the top left of the screen. You'll see a little button in the bottom left that looks like a speaker. Click on that and choose any sound from Scratch's library, record your own sound, choose a random surprise sound, or upload one from your computer.

Adding Sounds

There are three ways you can add sounds to your project. You can choose from one of the built-in sounds, you can record your own sound, or you can load a sound file from your computer.

If you go into the library of sounds and move your mouse over each one, you will hear a preview of that sound. Click on the sound to select it and add it to the currently selected sprite or stage.

Sound Library

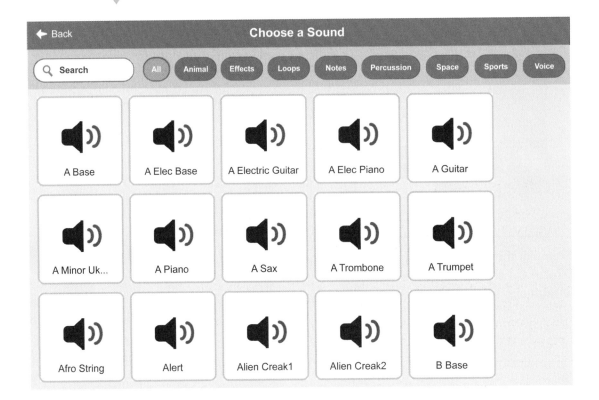

There are many different types of sound files that Scratch supports. Look for files that have MP3 or WAV at the end of their names. Those will most likely work.

You can also record your own sounds if your computer has a working microphone. You may need to allow Scratch to record your sounds. Always ask your parents or guardians before allowing any website, even Scratch, access to your computer.

Once you record your sound, it might look something like this.

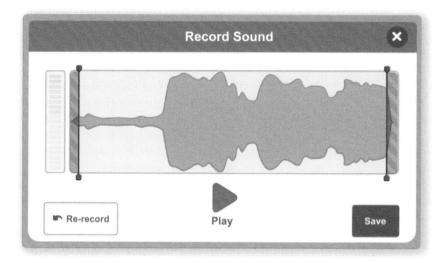

But before you can use it, you need to learn how to edit it.

Editing Sounds

You don't have to stick to just adding or recording sounds. You can also change them! To learn how to do this, you need to first understand what that pink box with the lines in it does. That box shows the volume of the sound as it plays. The left side is the start of the sound and the right side is the end. This helps you "see" the sound. If you look closely as the sound plays, you can usually see where different parts of it start and finish. This will help you choose which parts to change.

Volume View

The *Trim* button above the pink box lets you change the name of your sound or take out parts of it. When you click on it, you'll see two red bars show up, which you can move left and right. Anything between those two red lines will stay, but anything that's in the red-and-orange-colored section will be deleted. This way you can make your sounds shorter if you want so you can get exactly the sound you want. You can also rename your sound here to something more meaningful to you.

Sound Editor

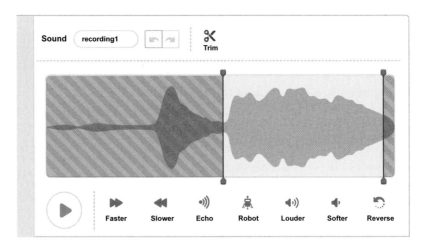

You can also make permanent changes to a sound here, like making it faster, slower, louder, or softer; adding an echo; making it sound like a robot; or even playing it backward. You'll learn more about these a little later in the chapter but try them out now anyway. You can combine these changes as well. Don't worry if you mess up. You can always click the *Undo* button (which looks like a curved arrow pointing to the left) or *Redo* button (which looks like a curved arrow pointing to the right) to the left of the *Trim* button.

MANY SPRITES ARE ALREADY PAIRED WITH THEIR OWN SOUNDS.

The Sound Blocks

Now that you know how to add and edit sounds to make them your own, it's time to learn about the different Sound blocks! These blocks can do a whole bunch of really fun things. They can play funny noises, make them louder or quieter, and even make them sound really squeaky like a mouse! They remember any changes you make, so you can do things like make the sound for one sprite louder than the others!

You might think that you can only use the premade sounds Scratch has built in. After all, it makes sense that all the sounds would be in the Sounds tab. But that's not true! There are some more advanced blocks in the Music extension that let you do things like play instruments and speed up the sound. Don't worry too much about these blocks right now, though. Focus on learning the core Sound blocks, and by the time you run into the Music blocks in Chapter 11, you'll be a pro at using sound in your projects!

Playing Sounds—The Fun Part

The easiest way to get started with sounds is to add the "start sound _____" or "play sound _____ until done" block.

These two blocks are pretty similar. They both start to play a sound! They are a little different though. The "play sound _____ until done" block finishes the entire sound before playing the next block. The "start sound _____" block just starts the sound and then goes to the next block right away. This can sometimes make two sounds play at the same time if they're right after each other.

Here's an example. Try adding the blocks in the following diagram to a sprite in your project and listen to the sounds. It's okay if you use different sounds than these. Choose whatever sounds you like.

You should hear the first block play the "<u>Birthday Bells</u>" sound until it finishes on its own. The next block, "start sound <u>Alien Creak2</u>," starts the sound but doesn't wait for it to finish playing. So the very next block, "start sound <u>meow</u>," happens at almost the same time! You can add a lot of "start sound _____" blocks together to create some crazy new sounds!

stop all sounds

Sometimes you have a really long sound that goes on for a while, like music playing in the background. But when Scratch finishes the current set of blocks, you don't always want that music to keep playing. That's what the "stop all sounds" block is for. It stops any sound that's playing and moves on to the next block, if there is one.

Keep It Down!

Just like each sprite has an *x* and *y* variable, each sprite and the stage as a whole has a current *sound* variable called "volume." Underneath the Sound blocks, you'll see a round block that says "volume" with a white box next to it. If you click on that checkbox, you will see the volume for that sprite or stage.

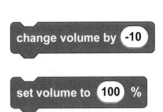

You can permanently make a sound louder or softer in the sound editor under the *Sounds* tab by clicking on the *Louder* and *Softer* buttons. You'll even see the size of the sound change! If you don't want to change the sound permanently, you can also change the volume using the "change volume by _____" and "set volume to _____%" blocks. When you use these blocks, they change the volume for only a little while when you run the blocks of code.

▶ CHANGING SOUND EFFECTS

You don't have to just play the same old sounds that Scratch gives you. You can also make your own sound effects in Scratch! There are a whole bunch of different effects that you can add on to make really cool and completely new sounds!

Just like with other blocks, you can change or set how much of an effect you use. The "change _____ effect by _____" block lets you make the pitch or other effect bigger or smaller and the "set _____ effect to _____" block sets it to a specific level. Remember that these changes don't permanently change your sound the way the changes you make in the sound editor do.

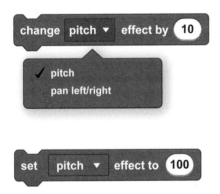

FACT

Pitch

The *pitch* of a sound is how high or low it is. If you increase the "pitch effect" on a sound, it will start to sound like a squeaky mouse. The sound also plays faster as the pitch goes up. If you lower the pitch, it will make the sound really deep and scary. It will also slow down the sound and make it play for a longer time.

Try out these example blocks. They'll change the pitch by twenty each time. When you click the green flag, you'll hear it get higher and higher! If you want it to get lower, change the 20 to –20!

You can do the same thing with the "pan left/right effect." Higher numbers make the sound shift more toward the right speaker while lower numbers make it sound like it's coming from the left speaker. You won't notice this effect unless you have two speakers far apart or if you're using headphones though.

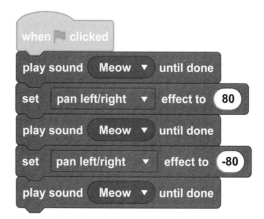

If you want to go back to the original sound before you made changes with the Sound blocks, you can use the "clear sound effects" block. The "clear sound effects" block will take away all of the effects of your Sound blocks, making it just like it was before any of these changes. This won't take away any of the effects you made in the sound editor though.

```
clear sound effects
```

In the sound editor, you can make permanent changes to a sound with a lot of different effects. Take a look at this list to see all of the different things you can do!

- **Faster/Slower**—These two make sounds squeakier (higher) or deeper (lower) in pitch. This doesn't change the volume though.
- **Echo**—This makes the sound repeat itself just a little bit, like you're in a tunnel. Use this to make music more ghostly sounding.
- **Robot**—This makes the sound really mechanical, like a robot is making it!
- **Louder/Softer**—These two change the volume of the sound to be higher or lower. You will see the size of the sound in the editor get bigger or smaller.
- **Reverse**—This changes the sound to play in reverse. Record saying your name and see what it sounds like in reverse. Creepy!

ESSENTIAL

When you change a sound with "effects" blocks, it's good practice to reset your sound back to what it was at the beginning by adding the blocks "clear sound effects" and "set volume to 100%" after a "green flag" block.

Activity | Party Tunes

★☆☆
EASY

In this activity, you'll get to connect different sprites that you click on to make different sounds.

Party Backdrop

1. Start the Background Music

Like always, start by adding a backdrop. You want some party tunes, so let's choose the Party backdrop! Now we need to add a sprite to make some noise. Add the keyboard sprite and go to its *Sounds* tab. Add a sound to the keyboard for some background music. One of the "Dance" sounds will work pretty well here.

Now you need to make the keyboard play the music when it's clicked. You don't want the music to be too loud when you first click the green flag to start your project since you're going to add some other sounds that can be played at the same time. Maybe try the "set volume to _____%" block to control that right from the start.

Next, you want to see that the music is actually playing. That means a costume change! Change the costume to "keyboard-b" so it looks like it's making some noise.

Now let's add a Sound block so it can play some music before changing back to the first costume. Which Sound block do you think we should use? Well, you want the entire sound to play before moving on to the next block, so maybe the "play sound _____ until done" block is the one you want.

This is great so far, but what if you want to change the pitch in the middle of the song? Well, you can add a yellow Events block you haven't seen yet called "when this sprite clicked." This makes it so the connected blocks start when you click on the keyboard. Add a "change <u>pitch</u> effect by _____" block to that and you can make it get higher whenever you want!

How are you doing with this activity? Following along? If so, your blocks for the keyboard should look like this.

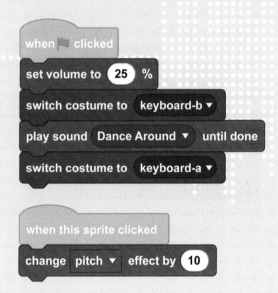

Try it out by clicking on the green flag and then click on the keyboard a couple of times. Sounds pretty awesome so far!

2. Add Extra Sounds

It'll sound even better if you can add in some more sounds with other sprites. You should add some drums! Grab a drum sprite and a drum cymbal sprite for this. Now add in the "switch costume to _____" and "play sound _____ until done" blocks just like you did for the keyboard, though this time you don't need to change the volume. Drums are supposed to be LOUD! You only want these to start when you click on them, so use the "when this sprite clicked" Hat block, not the "when green flag clicked" block.

3. Add a Drummer

The drums look a little strange on their own. Add a drummer like Casey to your sprites. You want him to be behind the drums so use the "go to <u>back</u> layer" block to send him there.

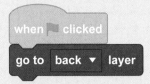

4. Record a Sound

You don't want Casey to stand quietly while everything else is playing but there isn't any "Yippee!" noise for him to make. But wait, you *can* make one! Record a sound with Casey to say something like "Yippee!" Don't forget to rename your recording to "Yippee!" Add some blocks so Casey says "Yippee!" while jumping up and down. Don't forget to add a blank "say _____" block at the end so he stops saying "Yippee!" Do your blocks look something like this?

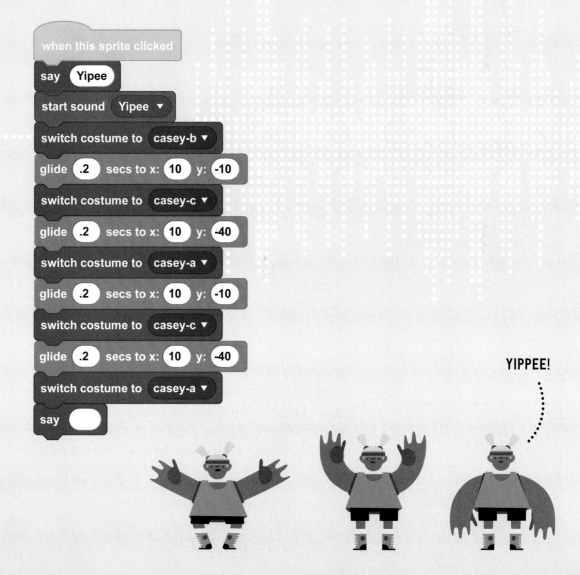

5. Change That Tune!

What if you want to change the background music? Well, you can add another sprite and select some different music for it to play! This example adds in a birthday cake. When the green flag is clicked, it will set the cake's costume so it doesn't look like the candles are lit. Then, when you click on the cake, all other sounds will stop and the candles will come on while "Happy Birthday" plays!

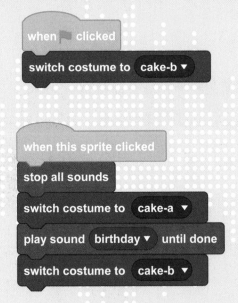

Add in as many other sprites as you like with different sounds to play!

6. Stop the Music!

Finally, you should make a way to stop all the music. After all, it can't play ALL the time. Add in another sprite that will let you stop everything, like Button5, the big *X* button sprite. This code should be pretty simple. All you need is the "when this sprite clicked" block and the "stop all sounds" block. Now when you click the *X* button, the music stops and the keyboard sprite changes back to its nonplaying costume.

```
when this sprite clicked
stop all sounds
```

5

EVENTS CHANGE THE WORLD

EVENTS

Events are happening all the time, all around the world. Sometimes events are for the start of something fun, like the opening ceremony of the Olympics. Sometimes events are to celebrate when something changes, like a birthday party. Sometimes events are just to tell a lot of people something important, like an assembly at school. Events in Scratch are like these events. Some Events blocks start the game, some of the Events blocks celebrate when something changes, and some tell other blocks something important. Let's learn about some of these Events blocks!

Understanding Events

Just like events in the real world, Scratch events can happen at any time. But unlike real-world events, you can control Scratch events! For example, if you put the "when green flag clicked" block on top of another block, the block will start only when you click the green flag. If no one clicks the green flag, then it never happens. All events in Scratch are like this—you have to do something to make the event happen.

You've already learned about blocks that are mostly rectangular with a little bump at the beginning and oval-shaped blocks. Now take a look at some yellow Events blocks. You should notice there are some blocks that look a little different. These special-shaped blocks are called *Hat blocks*, and they're the ones that let you start your events.

If you put blocks of code into the workspace without a Hat block, the only way those blocks will ever do anything is if you click on them. Otherwise they will just sit there and do nothing. You use these Hat blocks to get everything started at the right time. The Events blocks in Scratch all start with "when." When one of these things happens in Scratch, your Events block will begin to run your code blocks to make your sprite do what you want.

There are two different types of events that happen in Scratch. One type of event comes from the outside, from someone telling your project what to do. One example would be a player pressing the *up arrow* key to make a sprite jump. The other type of event, called an *inside event*, is one that you create. An example of this would be the "when backdrop switches to _____" event. This event is caused by other blocks inside your project switching the backdrop, not directly by the player.

HAT BLOCKS ARE THE
BLOCKS THAT LET YOU
············ START YOUR EVENTS.

Outside Events

How do you get a computer to do different things? The most common ways are from the mouse or the keyboard. You move the mouse around and click on things, or you press keys on the keyboard. In Scratch you can connect blocks to do things when someone presses a certain key or clicks something with the mouse. These are *outside events*. There are a few kinds of outside events in Scratch that you can use, like the "when green flag clicked" Events block. Here are all the different things that can happen to start outside events.

- The green flag is clicked.

  when ⚑ clicked

- A certain key is pressed.

- A sprite is clicked.

  when this sprite clicked

- The stage is clicked.

  when stage clicked

- A timer reaches a certain number of seconds since you pressed the green flag or the loudness (the sound from the microphone) is above a certain level.

YOU CAN PROBABLY FIGURE OUT HOW A LOT OF THESE BLOCKS WORK JUST BY READING THEM!

- When using video, the amount of motion on the camera is above a certain level. This one is a little more advanced than the rest. You can learn more about video in Chapter 11.

You can probably figure out how a lot of these work just by reading them! The "when green flag clicked" block will start any blocks beneath it when you press the green flag, the space bar (or any other key you'd like) will start any blocks beneath it when you press the indicated key, and so on. The "when timer > 10" block lets you delay something from happening for some number of seconds. Maybe you want your sprite to show up on the stage after ten seconds and say "Hello!" You can use this block to do that like this.

ESSENTIAL

Notice that you need to hide your sprite when you click the green flag so you won't see it right away.

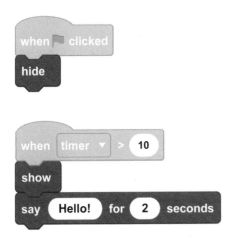

Inside Events

You can also make events happen when you want them to, not when the person playing the game presses a button. These are *inside events*, and you can make these events happen using other blocks.

The best way to understand an inside event is to see why you would need one in the first place. Imagine you have two sprites on your stage. They each have their own blocks that can make them do things, but they don't know what the other sprite is going to do. If you want them to do something at the same time, you have two choices:

1. You can add timing to make them do things just at the right time, like you did with the cat and the monkey in the *Tell a Story!* activity.
2. You can create an inside event so one sprite tells the other to do something.

when backdrop switches to   backdrop1 ▼

There are two inside event Hat blocks: "when backdrop switches to _____" and "when I receive _____." The "when backdrop switches to _____" block does exactly what it says. If you change the backdrop with the "switch backdrop to _____" Looks block, then any blocks connected to the "when backdrop switches to _____" block will begin to play.

when I receive   message1 ▼

broadcast   message1 ▼   broadcast   message1 ▼   and wait

Just like the "when backdrop switches to _____" block waits for the "switch backdrop to _____" Looks block to play before doing anything, the "when I receive _____" block waits for the "broadcast _____" or "broadcast _____ and wait" blocks before it does anything. These blocks send and receive messages. This message is just the name of the event. You can make up whatever name you want for it. An Events message isn't the same as the "say _____" or "think _____" blocks, which show a different kind of message. You can't see Events messages on the stage. They're sent from one sprite to another to tell it to do something.

These blocks also help you create new messages. If you click on the drop-down menu in any of those blocks, you'll see an option for "new message." You can name your message whatever you want. Get creative! Now that you know how to create a message, let's learn how you can use them.

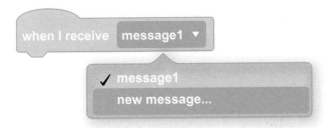

Timing Things with Messages

Where messages really help is when you have two sprites talking to each other. You don't want to have to hit a key or click a button every time you want to get to the next part. Instead you can make it so one sprite knows when the other one is talking to it!

In this example, Avery the adult is asking Becky the ballerina to show her a dance. After Avery asks "Can I see your dance routine?" the "broadcast <u>finished asking to dance</u>" block will send Becky the "<u>finished asking to dance</u>" message. If Becky's blocks begin with the "when I receive <u>finished asking to dance</u>" Hat block, Becky will start to dance by changing her costume twelve times when Avery broadcasts this message. The "repeat" block here simply repeats the blocks inside of it twelve times.

ALERT

You'll learn more about repeating in Chapter 7: Control.

She'll say "Sure!" and then begin to dance! After she's done dancing, her script will send the "ballerina dance done" message back to Avery. That will let Avery know that it's time to say "Thanks!"

The "broadcast _____" and "when I receive _____" blocks worked together to let each other know when one sprite wanted the other to start doing something. Messages can be a little tricky to understand, but once you get them, they can really make your games great!

Broadcast and Wait

You might have noticed a second block that looks a lot like the "broadcast _____" block. This is the "broadcast _____ and wait" block.

```
broadcast  message1 ▼  and wait
```

Any blocks you have after this block won't start until everything that received the message finish all of their blocks. This can sometimes make things a little simpler if the blocks you have don't need to keep going while something else is happening.

MESSAGES
CAN REALLY
MAKE YOUR
GAMES GREAT!

Take Avery and Becky, for example. Avery's second set of blocks don't start until after Becky finishes all of her dancing. Instead of sending and receiving a new message after Becky is done, you could just use the "broadcast finished asking to dance and wait" block and put the "say Thanks! for 2 seconds" block immediately after it.

when ⚑ clicked

say Can I see your dance routine? for 2 seconds

broadcast finished asking to dance ▼ and wait

say Thanks! for 2 seconds

Now Becky doesn't need to tell Avery that she has finished dancing since Avery is waiting until she is done, so we can take out the broadcast block from her code.

when I receive finished asking to dance ▼

say Sure! for 2 seconds

repeat 12

wait .1 seconds

next costume

Be careful using this block though. If the blocks that receive the message never finish, then the blocks after the receive will never happen either. If you add a "forever" block, which you'll learn more about in Chapter 7, around a few of Becky's blocks, then the last message from Avery to say "Thanks!" will never happen. Very impolite, Avery!

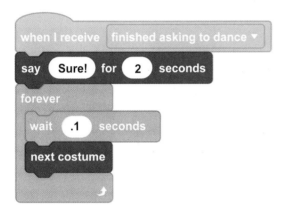

Parallel Events

Sometimes you can have one event, like clicking the green flag, start more than one script. This is possible using *parallel events*, or two things happening at the same time.

For example, take a look at the following two scripts. If they're both for the same sprite, when you click on that sprite, it will say the three speech bubbles and, at the same time, it will be dancing.

Activity | Dance Party!

MEDIUM

Now that we know how to control when events happen, let's make a story with different scenes! In this is activity, you are going tell a story of a boy playing his drum. Along the way, he'll look for a friend to play with and ask the friend to dance along with the music.

Spotlight Backdrop

That was SO MUCH FUN!

1. Set the Backdrops Up

For this project, you're going to want three different scenes. First the boy has to find a friend. Next he has to play his drum, and then everyone dances!

You are going to start by adding three different backdrops, one for each scene. Go with the Blue Sky backdrop when he's practicing, the Party backdrop when he finds a friend, and the Spotlight backdrop for the main event.

Next, we need to make sure the backdrops switch when we want them to. That sounds like an event! Make sure you've selected the backdrop for adding the blocks to. It should be highlighted with a blue border.

You need to start this with an Events Hat block so take the "when green flag clicked" block.

Now you want to add some Looks codes so the backdrops will change when you want them to. We want other blocks to run after the backdrops change, so let's go with the "switch backdrop to _____ and wait" block.

How are you doing? Following along? If you've gotten this far, your code should look like:

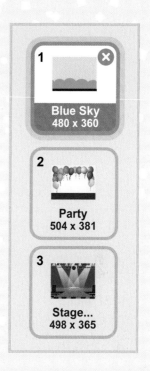

2. Choose Your Sprites

Now it's time to make your characters. In the first scene, the boy starts playing a drum. That means we need a sprite for the boy and a sprite for a drum! For this example, you should use the Devin and the Drum Kit sprites.

Now, let's make it so Devin plays the drums. First, let's change Devin to the "devin-d" costume to start. This costume makes him look like he's about to hit the drum.

Now you want him to say "I like beats!" so grab a "say _____ for _____ seconds" block and fill that in. You haven't seen "repeat" yet, but you'll learn more about this in Chapter 7. For now all you need to know is that this will make the "broadcast _____ and wait" block repeat ten times so we can get ten beats.

At the end of playing the beats, Devin says that it would be more fun with others, and that's the last of this group of blocks.

THIS WOULD
BE MORE
FUN WITH
OTHERS.

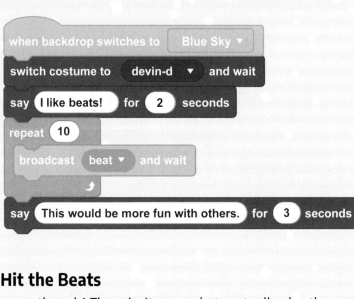

3. Hit the Beats

Hang on though! There isn't any code to actually play the sound. You'll need to add blocks to the Drum Kit sprite to make it play a drum beat each time it receives the broadcast message. How do you think you would do that?

A drummer's hands don't stay still when he's playing, so let's get his hands moving! Each time a beat happens, you can change the costume for Devin to make it look like he hits the drums. When Devin receives the "beat" message, he immediately switches to the costume with his hand down, waits 0.2 seconds, and then switches back.

If you want, you can make it look like the Drum Kit is playing music by changing costumes for a beat, the same way Devin did. Try out your project so far by clicking the green flag!

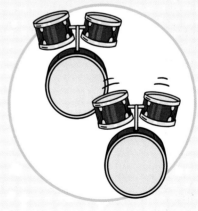

4. Find a Friend

Now you are ready to move to the second scene. First, you need to find a friend to dance, so go into the sprite library and find Devin a friend. This example uses Otto the Octopus, but any sprite with a couple of different costumes will work.

We don't want Otto to appear in the first scene, so let's hide him to start and then make him appear at the start of the second scene. What event means that the second scene is starting? The backdrop switching to the Party, of course! So let's use the "when backdrop switches to Party" block this time.

Otto is going to move around later on, so let's make sure that he turns up at the right place when he first shows up. Move him wherever you like for the Party backdrop and then drag out the "go to x: _____ y: _____" block. Now add a "show" block under it for him to turn up on time!

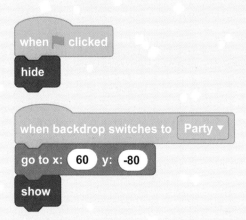

5. Switch to the Party Backdrop

Devin is kind of surprised to see Otto. After all, he's an octopus! Let's have him ask about it when Otto shows up. When does Otto show up? When the backdrop switches to Party. So you should start this code with a "when backdrop switches to Party" block. Then add a "say _____" block for Devin to ask "Who are you?" Well, you want Otto to answer when Devin asks, so Devin should broadcast a new message so Otto can introduce himself. After this, have Devin say "I have some beats for you" and broadcast the "beat" message again.

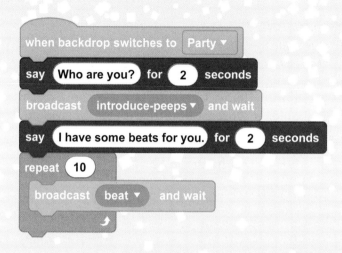

Now you need Otto to respond to Devin's message. Grab a "when I receive introduce-peeps" Hat block and add a "say _____ for _____ seconds" block. Now write in a message so Otto introduces himself to Devin.

Party Backdrop

Every time Otto receives the "beat" message, you want to change costumes so it looks like he's dancing. That means we need to start with another "when I receive _____" block and then use the "switch costumes to _____" block. In this case, Otto should switch from the "octopus-b" to the "octopus-a" costume. Now, you should see Otto dancing while Devin is playing the drum.

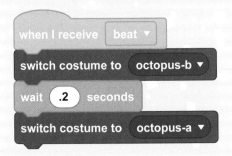

6. Switch to the Stage Backdrop

Once Devin is done playing, the backdrop blocks will switch to the final backdrop: "Spotlight-stage2." Have Devin say "It is time for the main show" when the backdrop changes and then play music again. At the end he should tell the player how happy he was to play the drum for him!

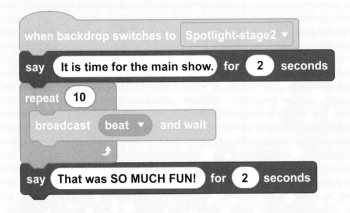

ALERT

If you want, you can add more sprites to dance; you just need to add the same blocks as you did for Otto the Octopus.

That's it! You made a dance party! Nice work!

6

OPERATORS CONNECT US ALL

OPERATORS

Think about math class. What do you learn? Addition, subtraction, maybe even multiplication and division! These are called *operations*, and you can do this math with codes too! You need to learn to use operators in Scratch so you too can perform just the right action to get what you need done. You might have to make something twice as big, or half as loud, or increase a score in your game. With Operators blocks you'll be able to do this and so much more.

What Is an Operator Anyway?

You've probably heard that adding two numbers together is called *addition*. Subtracting two numbers is *subtraction*. Both addition and subtraction are called *operations*. The symbols you use in these operations, like the "+" and "−" symbols, are known as *operators*.

Addition needs at least two numbers to operate on. After all, trying to add just one number doesn't make any sense at all! There are some Operators blocks, such as "round _____," that need only one number. There are even Operators blocks in Scratch that can do their job with words instead of numbers!

Operators blocks can be grouped together based on the types of things they can do. It is important to understand these groupings so you know the right situation to use them in. The first set of Operators blocks are our math operators.

BOTH ADDITION AND SUBTRACTION ARE CALLED OPERATIONS.

Math Operators

When you need to do some math in Scratch, the math Operators blocks have your back. Starting from the simpler ones, there are the "_____+_____," "_____−_____," "_____*_____," and "_____/_____" blocks. These are the blocks for addition, subtraction, multiplication, and division.

These Operators blocks are also called Reporter blocks. Just like a report card from school, they tell you (or whatever block they're in) the number they calculate. If you click on one of these math Operators blocks when they are by themselves, they don't have any other block to report the number to and so they'll just show it in a little bubble.

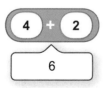

If you want to see the answer without having to click on it each time, you can put the operator inside a "say _____" block to have your sprite say the answer instead.

You don't have to use just one Operators block. The blocks can be combined together or stacked to create longer operations. For example, if you want to find out what 2*3*4 is, you can put an Operators block inside of another Operators block like this.

You might have learned in school that there's a certain order you have to do math operations in. If you do them out of order, it might create different answers!

For example, let's look at a simple equation like 2+3*4. What do you think the answer is? Did you guess 20? Sorry, it's 14, but good try! If you do this operation by adding 2 and 3 together first, you'd get 5. And then if you multiply by 4, you'd get 20.

But math has rules about what order to do everything in. First you do everything in parentheses. Then you do any exponents. Then you do all of the multiplication and division. Finally, you add or subtract whatever is left.

So let's look at that math problem again. The rules tell you to multiply before adding, so multiply 3 by 4. You should get 12. Now it's time to add the 2, and you end up with 14. That's not the same as 20!

Scratch helps you with this order when you stack blocks together. The way you stack them will determine which order it does these operations in. Let's take a look at that math equation again, this time using Scratch. If you put the "2+3" block inside of the "_____*4" block, it will add the numbers first and then multiply. If you put the "3*4" block inside of the "2+_____" block, it will multiply the numbers first.

ESSENTIAL

Think of it like the highest or topmost Operators block always goes first, then the next block under it would go, and so on until the end of the script.

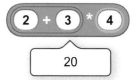

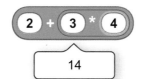

Besides the four normal math Operators blocks, there are a few others. The "round _____" Operators block rounds whatever number you put in to the nearest whole number. That means it gets rid of any decimal part of a number. Any number that has a decimal between .0 and .49 will be rounded down so you don't see the decimal point. For example, 10.25 would be rounded down to 10. Any number that has a decimal between 0.5 and 0.99 will be rounded up to the next closest number. So, for example, the number 10.75 would be rounded up to 11.

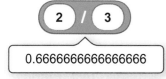

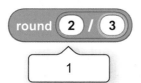

The "round _____" Operators block can be very helpful when used with a Sensing block or other math operations that have a lot of decimals that you don't want to show. For example, if you put the "timer" block inside the "round _____" block, it will count by the number of seconds instead of showing all those annoying parts after the decimal point changing like crazy!

When you play games, you might have noticed that some mobs of monsters have a lot of randomness to them. They seem to find their way to attack, but they don't go right to you. They kind of just wander in different directions. The "pick random _____ to _____" block can make your sprite do the same kind of thing.

pick random (1) to (10)

You can put things into random places, make them appear at random times, and much more. This is one of the most useful blocks in Scratch to make your projects more challenging and fun.

What if you needed a random number to include decimals? To get the "pick random _____ to _____" block to also pick decimals, all you have to do is put a decimal in the block! For example, if you want to get a decimal between 0 and 1, all you have to do is use "0.0" or "1.0" in your block.

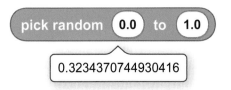

More Advanced Math Blocks

Now that you know some of the simpler math blocks, let's learn about some of the harder ones. Don't worry if you don't understand all of this. You'll learn about it at school as you get older.

The "_____ mod _____" block tells you what the remainder of two numbers would be if you divided them. For example, if you have "5 mod 2," Scratch will divide 5 by 2, which doesn't go evenly; 5 divided by 2 is 2 with a remainder of 1. Since this block is looking only for the remainder, the answer for this operation is 1.

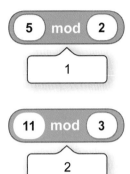

Let's try another example, since this can be a little confusing. If we used a block that said "11 mod 3," what do you think it would tell us? Well, 3 goes into 11 three times and then there's still 2 left over. That means the answer in this case is 2.

The "_____ mod _____" block can be very useful when you need to put things into groups. The "mod" function helps you work out what leftovers you will have. As an example, if you had fifty-two things and you needed to put them in groups of ten, you would have two left over. So "52 mod 10" is 2.

The "_____ of _____" Operators block is a really powerful block that can do many advanced math functions. This block has a list of different operations that you can use. Don't worry too much if you don't understand these. There are some really fancy math operations here, some that you won't learn about until you're much older. A couple you won't learn about until you're in high school! Here's the full list, a short explanation, an example of each one, and when you might use this block in the future.

ESSENTIAL

Coding often requires you to look up how to do things on the Internet. These blocks are there in case someone with a little more experience tells you to use it. Once you learn about these functions, you can come back and use them in Scratch!

Operator	What does it do?	Examples	Example project
abs	The absolute value of a number. This turns negative numbers to positive numbers.	"abs –3"=3 "abs 3"=3	Work out how far from the center of the stage a sprite is.
floor	Rounds the number down, no matter what its decimal is.	"floor 2.35"=2 "floor 0.99"=0 "floor –1.5"= –2	Various uses when you end up with fractions.
ceiling	Rounds the number up, no matter what its decimal is.	"ceiling 2.35"=3 "ceiling 0.99"=1 "ceiling –1.5"= –1	Various uses when you end up with fractions.
sqrt	Finds the square root of a number.	"sqrt 4"=2 "sqrt 3"=1.73	Calculate the distance between two points.
sin, cos, tan, asin, acos, atan	Trigonometry functions (usually taught around grade 10) for working with angles.	"tan 45"=1 "atan 1"=45 "cos 30"=0.866 "acos 0.866"=30	Draw curves or calculate trajectory of falling objects.
ln	The natural log.	"ln 7.389"=2 "ln 2.718"=1 "ln 1"=0	Helps work out how long it takes for something to grow.
log	Log to base 10.	"log 100"=2 "log 1"=0	Sometimes you want to shrink large numbers in the same range. For example, going from 0 to 1,000 using log would instead go from 0 to 3.
e^	Amount of growth from an amount of time.	"e^ 2"=7.389 "e^ 1"=2.718	Helps figure out how fast something will grow.
10^	10 to the power.	"10^ 2"=100 "10^ 5"=100,000	Really useful when you get to really, really big numbers.

Don't worry too much about this block. You might find you rarely need to use it.

Conditional Operators

That's enough numbers for now. There are other types of operators that you can use from this section as well. Another type is *conditional operators*. Let's learn about them!

Conditional operators appear in the green hexagonal-shaped blocks in Scratch. They are also sometimes called *Boolean operators*, which is really fun to say. These blocks always report one of only two things. They report either something is *true* or something is *false*. Did you ever play the game *Twenty Questions*, where you had to try to guess what someone is thinking of by asking *yes* or *no* questions like "Is it an animal?" Well, conditional operators work the same way.

There are two different types of conditional operators: ones that work with numbers and words, and ones that work only with other conditional operators.

CONDITIONAL OPERATORS REPORT EITHER SOMETHING IS *TRUE* OR SOMETHING IS *FALSE*.

Comparison Conditional Operators

The three conditional operators that work with numbers and words are known as *comparison conditional operators*. The first block asks if the first number is less than the second number. The second block checks to see if the two numbers are equal. And the third block checks if the first number is greater than the second number. For example, if you ask if 5 is less than 3 and click the block, it will tell you *false*.

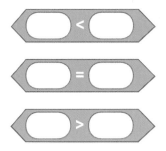

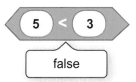

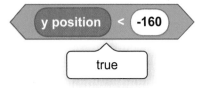

This is also useful for checking to see if things are close to the bottom of the screen. Why would you want to see if your sprite is close to the bottom of the screen? Well, maybe you created a game where your sprite is falling.

While it might seem like these blocks are good only for numbers, you can also compare words. This can be useful when you want to know if a variable is the right value. In this example it checks if the dragon sprite's costume is currently the "dragon-c" costume before it runs the "if/then" block. The "if/then" block here uses the operator to decide to do the "think _____ for _____ seconds" block that is inside the "if/then" block or not.

ALERT

You'll learn all about the "if/then" block in Chapter 7.

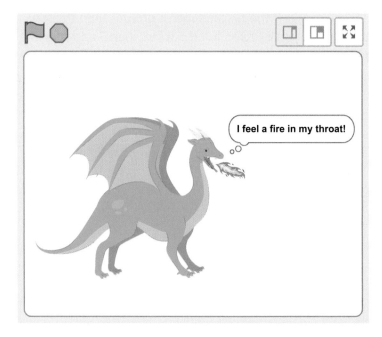

When you're putting words into these blocks, you don't have to worry about capitalizing letters. Scratch ignores upper- and lowercase letters and keeps them all the same. More advanced programming languages don't do this, so be careful if you start programming in Python or JavaScript.

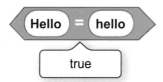

You can also use the comparison conditional operators to sort strings alphabetically. And in this case, cats are not greater than dogs! The word *cat* starts with a *c*, so it would come before (or is less than) the word *dog*.

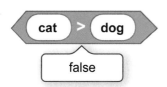

Logical Operators

The conditional operators reviewed so far can work with numbers and words. There are three other conditional operators that work only with other conditional operators. They're called *logical operators*: the "_____ and _____" block, the "_____ or _____" block, and the "not _____" block.

These first two blocks do exactly what you might expect. If someone tells you to clean your room *and* vacuum the stairs, you would understand that's different from someone saying to clean your room *or* vacuum the stairs. Scratch "_____ and _____" and "_____ or _____" blocks work the same way.

The "_____ and _____" block can combine other blocks to check if both conditions match what you need. For example, in this case we can check if the current sprite is wearing its first costume *and* if it's near the bottom of the screen.

The "not _____" block is useful to swap things around. If something is true, "not" makes it false. In the previous block you could add a "not" to the first part of the block, and it would check if the sprite is wearing its first costume and if it's not near the bottom of the screen.

not < y position < -160 > and < costume number ▼ = 1 >

Word Tricks

Often you will want to combine different words together for a sprite. It might be that you want it to say something that uses one of its variables, like its costume name here.

This block just connects two sets of words together. Anytime you have text or words instead of numbers, it's usually referred to as a *string*. There are two strings that join blocks. The first is the string "My costume is," and the second is the variable "costume name." Make sure to add a space at the end of the first string. If you don't, the two words will smoosh together!

There are three other blocks that also work with strings. The "letter _____ of _____" block finds the letter that is at a specific count in a string. So, for example, "letter 1 of world" would be the letter *w* and "letter 5 of world" would be *d*.

Sometimes you'll want to know how long your string is. The "length of _____" block tells you how many letters are in the string. In this example, the "length of world" is five.

The final block that works with strings is the "_____ contains _____?" block. This can be helpful if you need to know if a string is part of a different string. For example, let's say you have a sprite that has five costumes: "Charlie-1," "Charlie-2-bouncing-ball," "Charlie-3-dunking," "Charlie-4-holding-ball," and "Charlie-5-sitting." If you want to know if Charlie is currently wearing a costume with a ball, then you can use the "_____ contains _____" block to tell you.

Activity | *Math Jeopardy!*

EASY

In this activity you will get to create a math game to challenge your friends! Just like *Jeopardy!*, Ripley will give the answer and ask you for the question. You can put in a lot of distracting answers to make it harder, and each one that the player clicks on will show if it's right or wrong!

Space Backdrop Example

1. Add the Sprites

First add a sprite to give the player the question. Then add a backdrop to make it more fun. You can pull one from the Internet or use a background from Scratch. Let's use Ripley for this example. You want to make sure the player knows what to do, so have Ripley give some directions and then ask the question.

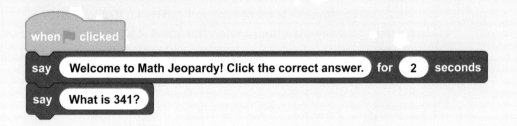

Click the *Paint* icon to draw your own sprite. Draw the costume with some text by clicking the *Text* icon and add your own math equation, such as "32*3" in the example. Do this a few times, making sure that only one equation is right.

2. Make the Wrong Answers Speak

Now you want to make a wrong answer tell the player that it's wrong if it's clicked on, so let's use a "when this sprite clicked" Hat block to get these blocks started. Now you need to attach a "say _____ for _____ seconds" block so the equation will tell the player he or she is wrong. In the first blank, you'll need to use some operators to tell the player what that equation actually equals. Which operators do you think you would use to tell the player that "11–5*10" is not the right answer? Well, you're going to want to join a text string with a number, so you'll want the "join _____ _____" block. In the first part, you can tell the player that's not the right answer with something like "It's not me. I am:." Then in the second part you can add the equation using Operators blocks so it will do the math for you!

MAKE SURE THAT ONLY ONE QUESTION IS RIGHT.

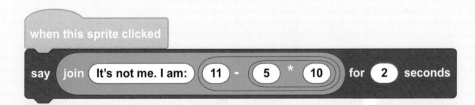

To make this a little more fun, you can make it so the wrong answers go away over time. When the game starts, you can have all of the answers show up and then wait a random number of seconds before hiding them.

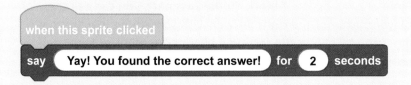

Do the same thing for each of the wrong answers. The more wrong answers you make, the more difficult it will be. But now you need to add the correct question. It would be pretty frustrating to play with no correct question!

3. Add a Right Answer

Add one more sprite with the correct question. This time, all you need is a simple block that tells the player he or she got it right!

Later on as you learn more blocks, you'll be able to come back to this activity and make it even more fun by using variables to ask more questions.

CONTROL THE FLOW

CONTROL

Have you ever played a game either online or in real life that had a treasure map? You had to find your way through a set of turns and obstacles following the directions. You had to make a lot of decisions based on where the map told you to go. In Scratch, Control blocks can let your sprites make decisions based on what's happening in the game. You will need them for all but the simplest projects. Sprites need to be able to think ahead on what you want them to do under many different conditions or when certain situations happen. To control all of this you need blocks that provide directions for your sprites. Control blocks are the way to do that.

Conditional Blocks

Have you ever asked your parents or guardians for something and they said, "Okay, but on one condition"? For you to get what you wanted, you had to do what they asked. One time they might have wanted you to clean your bedroom before you could go to a friend's house. Another time you might have had to finish eating your vegetables before you could have ice cream.

When you're building your game, you will often find that you have a set of blocks that you want to use, but only on one condition. For example, you might want to run a block only after the timer has run out or only if the player is pressing the *up arrow* key. That's a great time to use Conditional blocks. They run only when something else happens. You'll find yourself using a lot of new and interesting Conditional blocks, and every situation will be just a little bit different. Knowing all of the different blocks will help you know which one to use when you're in these different situations.

Some of the Control blocks need a hexagonal block added to them. This block that you add to it is called a *condition*. Conditions are either *yes* or *no* (sometimes *true* or *false*). For example, the "if/else" block decides which path to choose depending on the condition.

CONDITIONAL BLOCKS RUN ONLY WHEN SOMETHING ELSE HAPPENS.

The "If/Else" Block

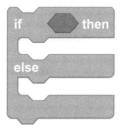

Let's look at the "if/else" block. It helps to decide what your sprite is going to do based on a condition you choose. If the condition is true, it will do whatever is in the first part. If the condition is false, it will do whatever is in the second part.

Say that you want to have a sprite switch back and forth between two specific costumes. To write this out as a normal sentence it might be: "If the sprite is displaying the second costume, then switch to the third costume or else (if not) switch back to the second costume."

You can do the same thing using the "if/else" block. The condition for this is "if the sprite is displaying the second costume," so you can use a "_____ = _____" Operators block to check if the costume number equals two. If it does, then you would want it to switch costumes, so add a "switch costume to _____" block in the first section. If it does not have the second costume on, you want it to switch back, so add a "switch costume to _____" block into the bottom section as well and choose the second costume from the drop-down menu.

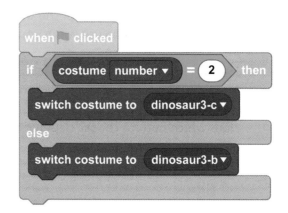

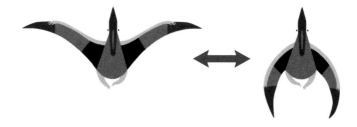

Scratch will ask if the current costume is the "number two" costume (or second costume). If it is, then the code tells the sprite to switch to "dinosaur3-c" (the third costume for this sprite); otherwise (or else) it will switch to dinosaur3-b (the second costume).

A good way to think about this is to picture the current costume for the dinosaur and go through the blocks in your mind. If, when starting, the dinosaur's current costume is the third costume, then when the condition (to see if the costume number is 2) is tested, it will be false.

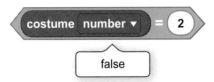

This means Scratch will perform the instructions for the blocks that are inside the "else" part of the "if/else" block. This switches the sprite to <u>dinosaur3-b</u>, the second costume. Now when you click the green flag next time, the current costume is the second costume, and so when the condition (to see if the costume number is 2) is tested it will be true and the sprite switches to <u>dinosaur3-c</u>, the third costume.

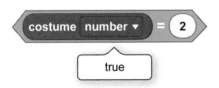

Sometimes it is easier to see this written out as a series of steps like this:

1. When you click the green flag
2. → if the current sprite's costume is the second costume then
3. → switch the current sprite's costume to the third costume
4. → else (if not)
5. → switch the current sprite's costume to the second costume

SOMETIMES IT IS EASIER TO SEE IF/ELSE WRITTEN OUT AS A SERIES OF STEPS.

The "If/Then" Block

The "if/else" block isn't the only type of Conditional block you'll use. The simplest one, and one you'll use often, is the plain "if/then" block.

You might notice that this looks a lot like the top part of the "if/else" block. It works the same way! The only difference is this block doesn't care what happens if the condition you make is false. It will just move on to the next set of blocks.

Let's take a look at an example in real life! Imagine your friend just texted and wants you to come to his or her house to hang out. When you ask your parents or guardians, they say, "If your room is clean, then you can go to your friend's house." You can go outside if, and only if, your room is clean. If it's not clean, then nothing special happens. You just aren't allowed to go outside.

This block is great when you don't want anything special to happen if the condition is false. For example, you might want to check if one sprite is touching another one but don't want to do anything special if the sprites are not touching. Or maybe you want to see if the current score is greater than the high score. If it is not a new high score, then you don't want to do anything special, but if it is, then you want a special message to appear.

The "Wait" Blocks

The "wait until _____" block does exactly what you might think it does. It waits until a condition is met, and then it does all of the blocks after it. Unlike the "if/then" block, "wait until _____" blocks stop Scratch from doing any of the other blocks until whatever condition you made is true.

You might notice there's another Control block that starts with "wait." It's not a Conditional block, but since you're learning about another block that waits, let's take a look at it.

The "wait _____ seconds" block is pretty simple. Instead of waiting for a condition like the "wait until _____" block, it just waits an exact amount of time! Sometimes you might need to wait a few seconds after an event happens, or maybe you just want to slow things down so they don't happen too quickly.

Loops

Everyone gets tired of doing the same thing over and over. It's so boring! Not for Scratch! It's happy to do something over and over and over and over, as many times as you want. It will even do some things over and over forever!

If there were no loop blocks, it might get really difficult to do something like this to change costumes over and over. The script would have to be really long (first example). There is an easier way though. Instead of repeating the same code, you can use the "repeat" block (second example).

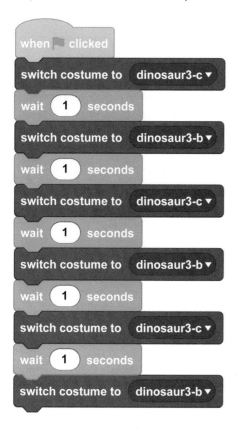
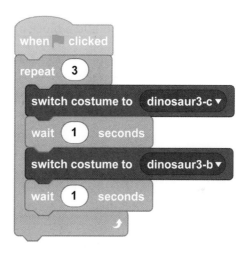

The "repeat" block lets you use exactly the right blocks you need without having to drag them in a bunch of times. It also lets you choose how many times you want to repeat before moving on to the next block. In this example, the original blocks repeated three times.

You won't always want to do actions a specific number of times. There is another block that will keep repeating the blocks inside over and over: the "forever" block. As you can imagine, this block causes Scratch to repeat the blocks contained inside forever. So if you have a situation where you always want to keep doing something from when the block starts to when you hit the red *stop* button, then the "forever" block is exactly what you need.

You will notice that you can't connect any blocks after a "forever" block. That's because this block never ends! You can't have a block run after it if this keeps going on and on and on and on forever! This is one of only a very few blocks that doesn't let you add a block after it.

Loops Inside of Loops

There is nothing stopping you from putting loop blocks inside of other loop blocks. There's even a name for it: *nested loops.*

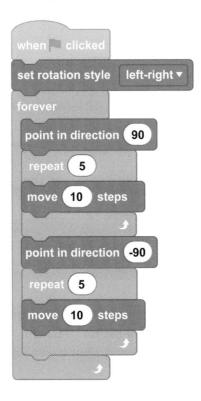

In this example, there are two "repeat" blocks inside of a "forever" block. Can you work out what this would do? It has a sprite point to the right and then move ten steps and repeats that five times. Then it makes the sprite point to the left and then move ten steps and repeat that five times. So a sprite would zip back and forth fifty steps going left and right, and because of the "forever" loop, it would keep doing that until you hit the red *stop* button.

A Loop and a Conditional Combined

There is one block that is both a loop and a Conditional block. The "repeat until _____" block makes it so that you can do something over and over until a certain condition is met. It's like the "wait until _____" block except instead of doing nothing until the condition is met, it just keeps repeating the blocks inside it. In the following example, you'll see a block you haven't learned about yet: "loudness." You'll learn more about this in Chapter 8. Once the microphone hears a loud sound, the "repeat until" block will stop and the next block after it will happen.

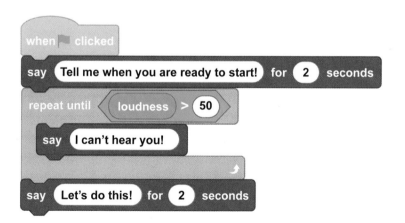

Another common practice is to put conditions inside of loops. This is necessary at times because Scratch evaluates a condition at only one point in time. If you want something to be checked or tested all of the time, then you need to put it inside a loop to check it over and over.

ALERT

If you don't add a condition to a Conditional block, it will act like the condition is always false! So a "repeat" or "repeat until _____" block without a condition will be the same as a "forever" block, an "if/then" block will never do the blocks inside of it, and an "if/else" block will always do the "else" section.

In this example, the blocks continually check the volume from the microphone. If it is over twenty, then the sprite will say, "Wow, that is loud!" Otherwise it says nothing. The difference here from the "repeat until _____" block is that the "forever" block keeps on going even after the condition is met.

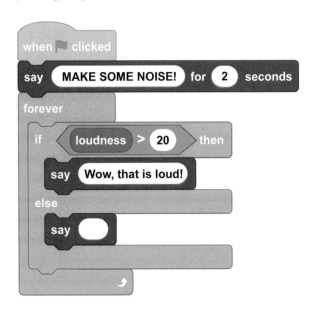

Stopping Blocks

At times in Scratch you will want to stop a set of blocks. This is a different type of control. Some things might take a long time to finish. You can decide to stop them from going any further with the "stop" block; Scratch stops any more blocks from happening.

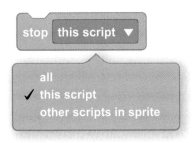

Do you have a "forever" block that you need to stop because something happened or a "repeat" block that's going on for a really long time? Or maybe you want all the other blocks to stop when you click on your sprite. There's no condition to check for this, so adding a "stop all" block after a "when this sprite clicked" Hat block lets you do that.

The different options in the drop-down menu of the "stop _____" block decides which set of blocks will be affected. "Stop all" does exactly what it sounds like. Every single script for every single sprite will stop.

"Stop this script" stops just the script attached to this block. Any other scripts you have running will just keep going. For example, maybe you have a game where more than one sprite bounces around a screen until you touch it with the mouse. You have to click on each one before the game ends.

> **ESSENTIAL**
>
> "Stop all" works the same way as the red *stop* button.

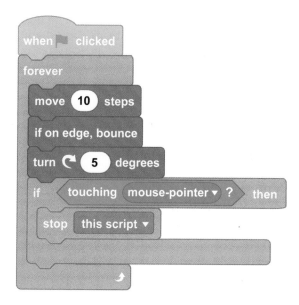

The "stop other scripts in sprite" block does the opposite of "stop this script." Instead of stopping all of the scripts on that sprite that the block is attached to, it stops all of the ones it isn't attached to! This can be useful when you have a main part of your code that you want to keep going, but want to stop other blocks from continuing.

Cloning

What would you do if you could create clones of yourself? Maybe one clone could do your chores, and another could go to school for you! And why not to do some babysitting and make some money for you to spend? What would you have your clones do?

In Scratch, clones can be super helpful as well. If you need a sprite to do something that's really close to what another sprite is doing, a clone can make things easier. It might be harder at first to get it working, but you'll be so happy you brought in the clones. They make it easier for you to fix problems in your code and usually in way fewer blocks than you'd normally need. Don't be afraid to create clones in Scratch!

Why Clones?

What would you want a clone for in Scratch? Well, what if you want to create an ant farm simulation? Would you create fifty different ant sprites? This sounds really boring. Here's an example of an ant farm simulation.

A Reason to Clone

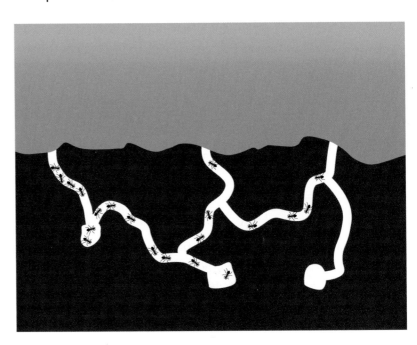

See all those little ants? It would be very hard to try to create this many sprites. And each one would need a lot of blocks copied into each sprite to make this happen. Cloning makes it so much easier in Scratch. So how do you do that?

Making Clones

There are three main blocks for making clones: "when I start as a clone," "create clone of _____," and "delete this clone."

To create clones of the current sprite, use the "create clone of myself" block. Well duh, that makes sense! This makes a copy of everything about the current sprite. And that really does mean everything: the current position on the stage, any graphic effects, its costume, if it's shown or hidden, and much, much more.

That doesn't mean the sprites always have to do exactly the same thing. What would be the point? Let's take a look at an example of how a cloned sprite can be different from the first one. Start a new project and add the Ballerina sprite. Now add the following blocks.

```
when 🚩 clicked
go to x: -190  y: 0
repeat 5
    create clone of myself ▼
    move 75 steps
    change color ▼ effect by 25
```

The first block moves them to the far left and then has a loop that does something five times by creating a clone each time, moving to the right and changing the color of the sprite. Try doing this too!

This will make six ballerinas show up on the stage. Why six? You have created five clones of the original sprite. So you'll have the five clones, plus the original sprite is still here.

EACH OF THE CLONED SPRITES IS CAPABLE OF DOING ITS OWN SCRATCH BLOCKS.

When I Start As a Clone

Each of the cloned sprites is capable of doing its own Scratch blocks. That's what the "when I start as a clone" Hat block is for! This gives a new script to each cloned sprite! Let's use that for our ballerinas. Add this script to our sprite to give the clones something to do.

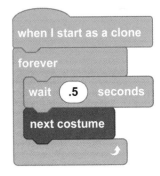

Take a look at all of the ballerinas dancing on your screen. Well, almost all of the dancers. Look at the original sprite all the way over on the right end. She's not dancing!

This is because it doesn't get to use the "when I start as a clone" blocks. There are a few different ways to fix this. The first is just to hide the main sprite after it makes its clones. That way there will be only the five cloned sprites visible, and they'll all be dancing! You have to add a show block when the clones start though. If you don't, you won't see them either.

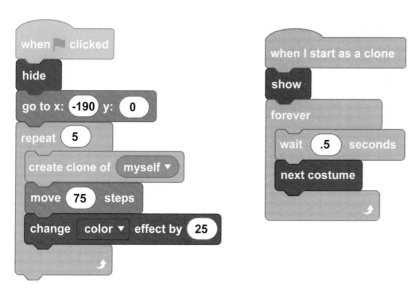

ALERT

Here's a hint: the only block under the "when I start as a clone" block should be your custom one.

The other way you could do it is to create a custom block. You'll learn about these in Chapter 10. You can make a block that tells all of the sprites to dance and add it on to the end of the original sprite's script. Then everyone's dancing together! Once you learn about custom blocks, come back here and see if you can figure out how to do this.

Another option is to broadcast a message. Then, instead of using the "when I start as a clone" Hat block, you can use the "when I receive _____" block. Send a message after creating all the clones. Because all clones have the same script as the main sprite, all of the clones will receive their own broadcast message and start dancing at the same time!

```
when [flag] clicked
hide
go to x: -190 y: 0
repeat 5
    create clone of myself ▼
    wait .5 seconds
    move 75 steps
    change color ▼ effect by 25
broadcast start dancing ▼
```

```
when I receive start dancing ▼
show
forever
    wait .5 seconds
    next costume
```

Activity | Forest Sim

EASY

In this activity you will get to create a forest of two different types of trees! You'll plant some new trees and watch as they grow and get old.

Jurassic Backdrop

1. Choose the Backdrop and the Sprites

First we need to choose a backdrop and then a couple of tree sprites. There are two tree sprites already built into Scratch: Tree1 and Trees.

2. Plant the Trees

Now go to the backdrop and add some code that creates new clones for the sprites each time you click on the stage. Start with a "when stage clicked" Hat block.

You want the code to do two different things: clone the Tree1 sprite and clone the Trees sprite. That sounds like a job for the "if/else" block! That way you can set a condition so sometimes it plants one and sometimes it plants the other.

ALERT

Remember, the "when stage clicked" block can be found only when you click on the stage in the sprite area.

Since you don't care which it plants, you should use a "pick random _____ to _____" block and just put "1" and "2" in the two blanks. That way the block will always choose between just the two options. Unfortunately, that's a Reporter block, which means it doesn't fit in the "if/else" block. But if you put it in a "_____ = _____" block, it should fit! Now set it to check if it equals "1."

Do you see what should happen with this code? The "pick random 1 to 2" block will choose either the number 1 or the number 2. If it's 1, it will clone Tree1, and if it's number 2, it will create a clone of Trees! Perfect!

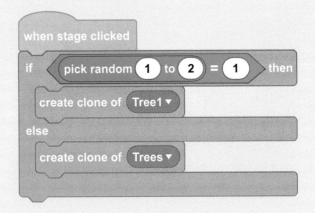

3. Control Where You Plant the Trees

You don't want to plant the trees in a random spot. You want to be able to control where you plant your trees! You should hide the first sprites when the game starts. Otherwise, there will be two trees that you didn't plant. That's a simple enough problem to fix. Just add a "hide" block to a "when green flag clicked" block on the two sprites, and they won't show up. Don't worry though. The clones you create still will.

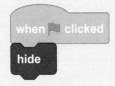

You want your trees to grow where you click the mouse. Click on one of the sprites and then go into the *Costumes* tab. Select all of the tree by clicking on each part and drag the tree up so the bottom of the sprite is in the center of the square. Now do the same thing with the other sprite.

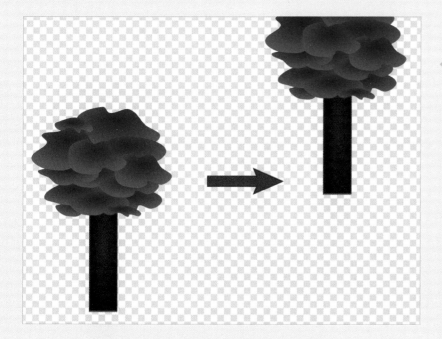

Repositioned Sprite

ESSENTIAL

A shortcut to put the same blocks into each sprite is to drag the blocks from one sprite over to the sprite area on top of the destination sprite that you want to move the code to as well.

Now you need to plant these trees! Add the Events Hat block for "when I start as a clone" since you want this code to happen each time a new tree is created. First you need to show the tree sprite and move it to where the mouse was clicked. To match where you have the mouse, it uses two Reporter blocks from the *Sensing* section: the "mouse x" and the "mouse y" blocks. Add these to a "go to x: _____ y: _____" block. This puts the tree clone exactly where you click the mouse.

4. Grow the Trees

When trees are first planted, they're usually pretty small so set the size of the clone to only 10 percent. Now you want the trees to grow. Use the "change size by 10" block to make it do that. But trees don't only grow once. Put a "repeat" block around it so it will grow a few times.

How many times should it grow? Well, some trees are bigger than others, right? You can make some trees grow more than others with a "pick random 5 to 10" block.

Once each tree finishes growing, it should wait a little while before continuing. After all, trees don't die right after they finish growing! You should add a "wait 5 seconds" block. Feel free to change this time if you like. Now it's an old tree though. Have it topple over by adding a turn to the right of ten degrees nine times. That makes ninety degrees, or just what is needed to get it to lie flat.

ALERT

Once the tree is lying on the ground, it should disappear, so add a hide block at the very end.

```
when I start as a clone
show
go to x: mouse x  y: mouse y
set size to 10 %
repeat  pick random 5 to 10
    change size by 10
wait 5 seconds
repeat 9
    turn ↻ 10 degrees
hide
```

SENSING IF THINGS CHANGE

SENSING

Do you know all of your five senses? You can see, hear, touch, smell, and taste. There might be even more than that! Just like you use your eyes, ears, fingers, nose, and mouth to experience the world, you use blocks in Scratch to tell if something is there or not! With these blocks, you can answer questions, like "What time is it right now?" or "Is the mouse currently touching my sprite?" or "Is my sprite touching the color *red*?" Sensing blocks are really important to help you make a fun game. Let's jump in!

What Are Sensors?

For people, our senses let us know when something is happening so we can react in the right way. For example, if your skin senses that the oven is hot, you will pull your hand away. It works the same way for Sensing blocks in Scratch! You will use Sensing blocks to help your sprites understand and react to the stage around them. That might mean they change directions when another sprite gets too close or they say something when they hit the wall of a maze. When talking about coding, *sensors* refer to the first two types of blocks that give back either *true* or *false* for Conditional blocks or words or number values for Reporter blocks.

One of the best methods of understanding these blocks is to click on them. You don't even need to drag them into the workspace to do this. Any block you click on will show you what the current value is. In these two examples, clicking on the "current hour" block will show the current hour of the day in a little balloon below the block, and clicking on the "touching edge" block will show *false* if the current sprite is not touching the edge of the stage.

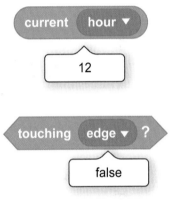

These are the values that these Sensing blocks will report or provide to whatever block you might put them inside of. You might decide to have your sprite say the current hour in a speech bubble or make a sound and change direction for a sprite bouncing around the screen. It is up to you to decide where you put the Sensing blocks depending on what you are trying to do.

There are different groups of Sensing blocks that you can use depending on the type of information that you need. You will want to think about someone playing your project and what type of control the player should have. As you think about this, you'll start to make some decisions about what Sensing blocks you need and at what times you will want to get this information.

YOU WILL USE SENSING BLOCKS TO HELP YOUR SPRITES UNDERSTAND AND REACT TO THE STAGE AROUND THEM.

Catch the Mouse!

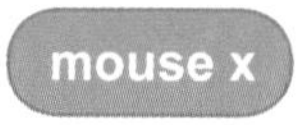
mouse x

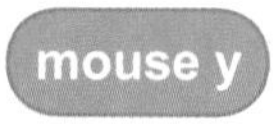
mouse y

The simplest thing you can make your sprite sense is where the computer mouse is. In Chapter 2, you learned about the "go to ______" block, which included a way to make the sprite follow the mouse pointer. You can do the same thing with the "go to x: ______ y: ______" Motion block and two Sensing blocks: "mouse x" and "mouse y."

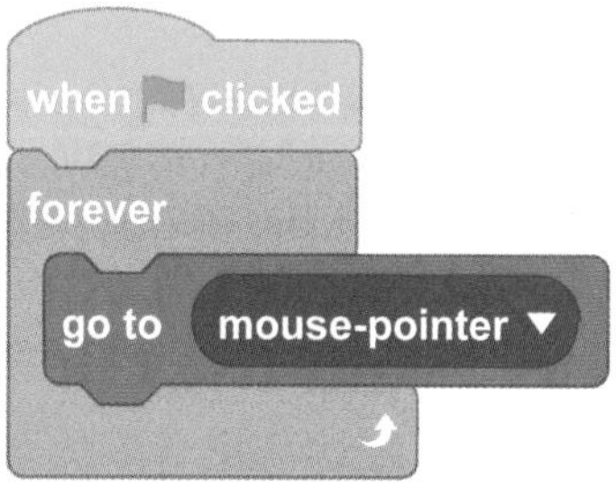
when clicked
forever
go to mouse-pointer

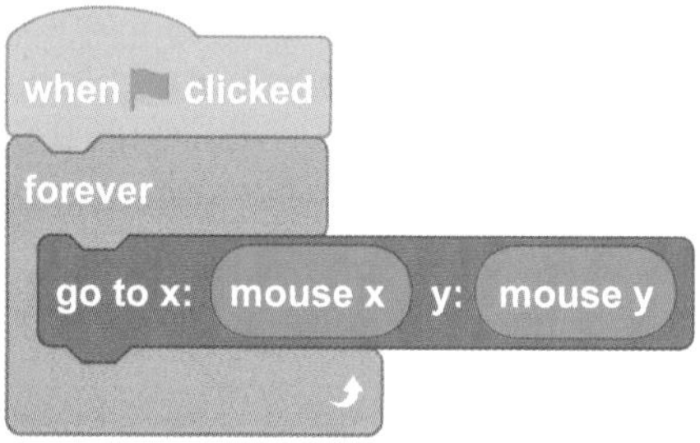
when clicked
forever
go to x: mouse x y: mouse y

ESSENTIAL

Did you notice in this example that the "mouse x" Reporter block and the "y position" Reporter block are very similar? The "y position" is really just another sensor that is specific to the current sprite! It's more closely related to where the sprite is, so Scratch puts it in the Motion category instead of the Sensing category of blocks.

You might be wondering why you would ever use the second way if it does the same thing and uses more blocks. Well, what if you want your sprite to not move up or down but you want it to follow the mouse left or right? You can do this by keeping the *y* value (up and down) the same for the sprite and change only the *x* value (left and right) to match the mouse position.

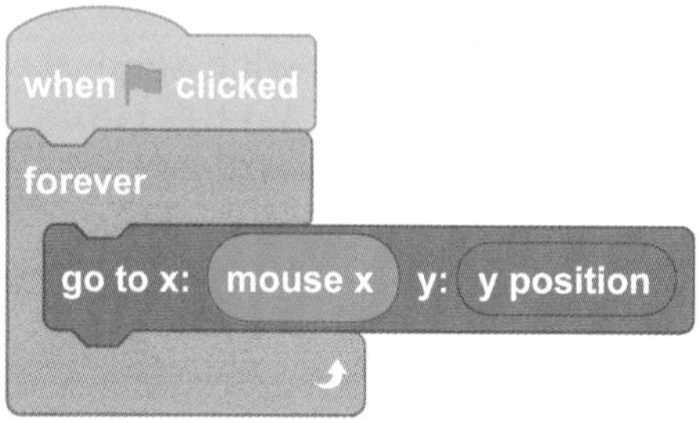
when clicked
forever
go to x: mouse x y: y position

You can sense more about the mouse than just where it is on the screen. Take a look at the "mouse down?" block.

mouse down?

This senses whether the person playing your project is pressing the mouse button or not. You can use this together with a loop with some condition that waits for the mouse button to stop being clicked. In the following example the loop will repeatedly check if the mouse is pressed or not. If it is, the sprite will start moving around the screen and changing costumes. If the mouse is not pressed, the sprite will just follow the mouse around the stage. This allows you to move the sprite wherever you want and then press the mouse key to have it start animating from there.

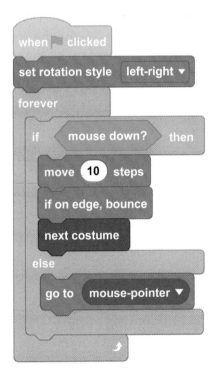

ALERT

There are a few things to watch out for when using the "mouse down?" block. You need to test how it works in the player mode (remember that when you click the *zoom* button on the stage, it goes to player mode), not just the regular view, since the mouse behaves slightly differently between the two.

On the stage you can drag your sprites wherever you want. The block "set drag mode _____" can change this in the player (zoom) view. If you set a sprite to be "not draggable," then you won't be able to drag it around in the player view. It will stay exactly where its blocks tell it to.

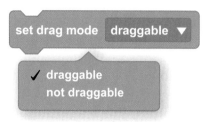

You can make your project sense more than just the mouse though. It can also sense the keyboard!

The Keyboard

Gaming can be a lot of fun when you use the keyboard to move around the screen. Maybe you want to use the space bar to have a character jump or use the *arrow* keys to move around. The "key _____ pressed?" Conditional block will let you use any key you want to control your sprite!

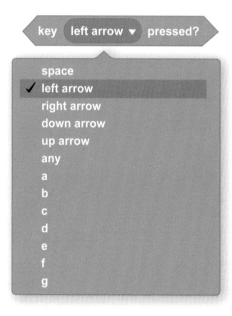

You might wonder how this block is different from the "when _____ key pressed" Events block. The Events block works similar to typing words into a document. If you press and hold down on a key, it repeats itself, but very slowly. That's perfectly fine sometimes, but if you want to control a sprite's movement on the screen, it will look a little rough. To get a smoother movement for your character, you will have to put the sensors for the direction keys inside a "forever" block and use the "if/then" Conditional block.

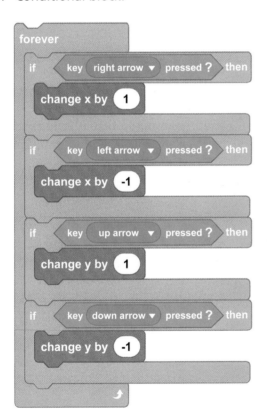

This will cause a sprite to move around the screen much more smoothly since the "forever" block will run as fast as possible on the computer.

Another difference between the "when _____ key pressed" block and the "key _____ pressed?" block is that you can press on more than one key at the same time with the Sensing block and both will activate. That means that if you pressed the *up* and *left arrow* keys at the same time in the previous example, your sprite would "change x by –10" (because you pressed the *left* key) and "change y by 10" (because you pressed the *up* key). Which way do you think the sprite would move? It would move diagonally up and to the left! You can't do this with the "when _____ key pressed" Events block!

Sometimes you might want something to happen each time there is a full key press and release. For example, perhaps you have a key that changes the backdrop in a loop. If you don't wait for the key to be released, the loop will immediately cycle through all the backdrops. You could do this same code with an event loop, but sometimes it might be easier to do a sequence of key press checks to create a chain of actions that happen on each key press.

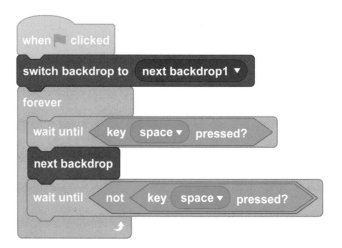

This will cycle through only one backdrop on each key press, even if you hold down the key, as it has to wait for the key to not be pressed.

The examples so far have used specific keys for the "key _____ pressed?" block. It's also possible to wait for any key to be pressed. This is a special option for the "key _____ pressed?" block. The "key <u>any</u> pressed?" block works in the same way as any other "key _____ pressed?" block except it activates when any key at all is pressed. You might use this to wait for any key to be pressed to start a game or perhaps to switch to a new level or backdrop.

Touch

If you are working with a touchscreen, your finger becomes the mouse. That means any code blocks that refer to the mouse (such as "when this sprite clicked" or "mouse down?") will start when your finger touches the screen. This is very similar to the mouse, but there are a few other things you need to consider that are special with touchscreens. Since there is no mouse, trying to use the mouse movement when the mouse is not pressed isn't possible. It will always be down or there will be no mouse movement at all for a touchscreen. If you have a project that you want to work on using a touchscreen, make sure to try it out on the touchscreen device. Also, on many touchscreens, there is no physical keyboard, so using the "key pressed" blocks won't work.

Collision Detection

Scratch doesn't only sense when a key is pressed. It can also tell if two sprites touch each other and if a sprite touches the mouse, the edge, or even a specific color on the screen.

Touching _____?

The "touching _____?" Condition block will report either *true* or *false* depending on whether or not the current sprite is touching whatever you choose in the drop-down list.

> **FACT**
>
> **Collision Detection**
>
> When sprites touch each other in games, it's usually called *collision detection*. That's a fancy way of saying it can tell when two sprites run into each other.

For example, a very common use for the "touching mouse-pointer?" block is to change a sprite's costume when you touch it with the mouse. Let's say you have a button in your project that shows the project instructions. You can make it so the button will change colors when you put the mouse over it, so the player knows that it can be clicked on.

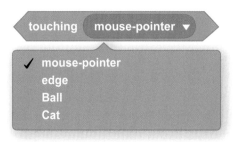

You can also use this block to check if the sprite is touching the edge of the stage or another sprite. If the sprite touches a specific sprite, maybe that means the player lost and you can add a sound and a message to let the player know. Or maybe touching the edge could mean the player won and gets to go to another screen in a platformer game.

Touching Colors

There are two more blocks that check if your sprite is touching something else. Instead of seeing if the sprite is touching a specific object, like the mouse pointer or another sprite, this block checks to see if your sprite is touching a specific color.

The "touching color _____?" block activates when the sprite touches the chosen color. The "color _____ is touching _____?" block looks for the first color in the current sprite and senses if it is touching the other color in another sprite or in the backdrop.

There are many ways to use these blocks! Let's start by looking at a few ways to use the "touching color _____?" block. The "touching color _____?" block is often used to make a maze or platformer game so you can check if the current sprite runs into a wall. You can also make a special colored door for an exit to the level. For example, you can make this maze. If the sprite touches the blue wall, it loses, and if it touches the pink door, it goes on to the next level.

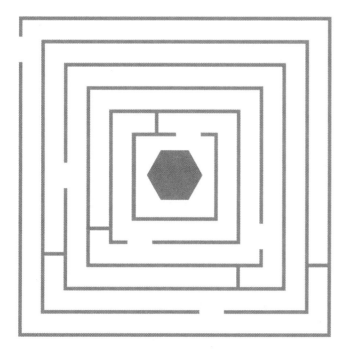

Maze

ESSENTIAL

Sometimes images have a lot of colors that look really, really similar but are not the same. However, this can make it difficult for the "touching color _____?" and "color _____ is touching _____?" blocks to work. One of the most common bugs in Scratch is when your script is checking for a similar color in a sprite that is made up of many different shades. It will detect only one of the shades and may even look like it's not working!

The "color _____ is touching _____?" block can do even more! You can pick any color in a sprite and know if it's touching some other part of a different sprite. It's helpful to draw your own sprites so you know exactly what color you're checking for.

This is also a great help when you build a maze. By adding a single pixel that's the same color as the background to each side of the sprite, you can build a four-way sensor that can detect if the sprite is about to run into a maze wall. If the dot hits the wall's color, you can tell the sprite to stop or move backward! For example, you could use a script like this to stop your sprite from running into a red wall.

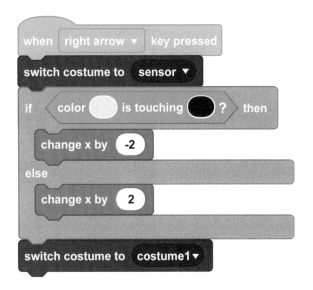

You can add dots to the top, left, and bottom of your sprite as well so it can sense any walls on those sides too. But it might look ugly if the player saw these dots. Use a color really close to the background for these dots, but not exactly the same.

You can also do it another way! Create your own costume for your sprite that is simply a colored box. Make it the same size as your sprite. Now you can have your sprite switch to that costume, sense if the color is touching the color of the maze, and then switch the costume back. It happens so fast you won't even notice the costume change!

If you need to notice when your sprite touches a wall, you can make all the borders the same color. But sometimes you will want to know which side the sprite touches. For example, if you make a platformer game and your sprite needs to fall to the ground, you would need to know if it is touching at the bottom versus the top or left or right. You could add something like this sensor costume and code to make it work.

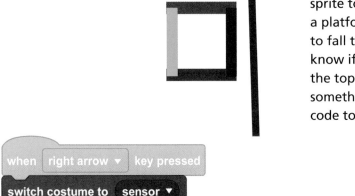

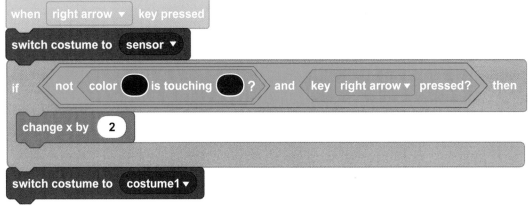

Take a look at that box where you choose your color.
You'll notice three bars: *Color*, *Saturation*, and *Brightness*:

- The *Color* bar is pretty easy to understand. That's where you choose your color.
- The *Saturation* controls how pure your color is. Zero means you won't even see the color. It will just be a dull gray, and 100 means it will be pure color.
- The *Brightness* controls how dark the color is. Zero will be totally black, and 100 makes the color as bright as possible.

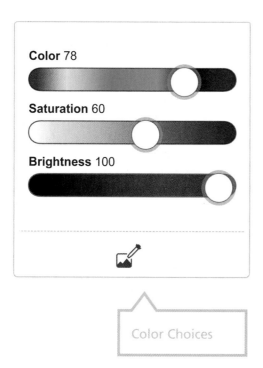

Color Choices

FACT

Saturation

Saturation controls how pure your color is. Zero will be totally washed out, and 100 will be a pure color.

Brightness

Brightness controls the amount of white or black in your color. Zero will be totally black, and 100 will be full brightness.

Just Once or All the Time?

Sometimes you might want to make your code check if two sprites are touching only when something happens. At other times, you might want to always be checking to see if your sprite is touching something.

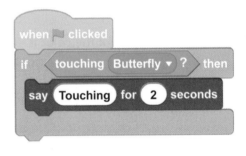

SOMETIMES YOU MIGHT WANT TO MAKE YOUR CODE CHECK IF TWO SPRITES ARE TOUCHING.

Take a look at these two codes. Both of them are checking if the current sprite is touching the butterfly when you press the green flag. But in the first one, there is no loop. That means if the two sprites are not touching when the green flag is clicked, then the code finishes and never checks to see if they are touching again. Even if they touch later, this code will be done, so it won't notice they are touching.

The second set of blocks always looks to see if the current sprite is touching the butterfly by using a "forever" block. Since the current sprite is also set to "move 10 steps" inside the "forever" block, the sprite will check to see if it's touching the butterfly every time it moves, and if it comes into contact with the butterfly, it will notice and say "Touching" for two seconds.

Distances

What happens if you want two sprites to notice if they're getting close to something else but not touching? Well, there's a block that will tell you how far away your sprite is from that object! The "distance to _____" block tells you and your sprite how far away it is from other sprites or the mouse pointer.

For example, if two sprites get too close together, maybe you want them to blush! How would you do that? You can use the "distance to _____" block to see how far away from each other two sprites are. In this example, the sprite changes color depending on how close it is to another sprite.

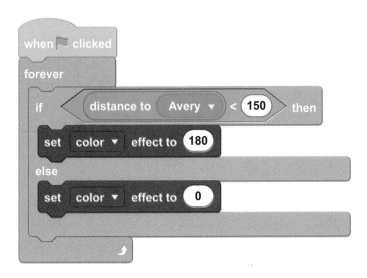

You can also use the "distance to mouse-pointer" option to see how close the mouse pointer is to a sprite. This example changes the sprite to get larger depending on how close the mouse is, but you could use this whenever you want something to happen based on how close the mouse is to a sprite.

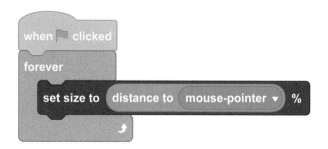

Dates and Time

In *Alice in Wonderland*, the White Rabbit was always running late! You're in luck though because Scratch has some blocks that will always keep you on time! They can tell you the date today, how much time has passed since you started a game, or even how many days there have been since January 1, 2000! Let's learn about a few of these blocks.

Current Date and Time Block

The "current _____" block can tell your sprite what the current year, month, date, hour, minute, second, or day of the week it is right when the block activates.

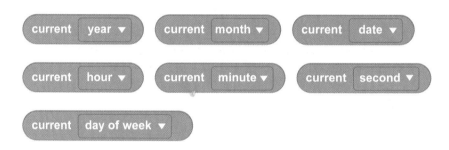

You might find it useful to use these blocks in games where you ask for someone's birthday and want to work out how many years old the person is or just to show the date and time in different ways. You can even have your sprites do different things on different days. Maybe you'll have your sprite look upset on Monday because the sprite has to go to school!

The "day of week" selection is a little weird. It reports the day as a number, with Sunday being the number *one* and Saturday being number *seven*. The best way to show the actual day of the week instead of the number is to make a list and then use a special Variables block. You'll learn more about how to do this in Chapter 9.

Timer Block

What if you want to make a game that gives more points the longer someone is able to play? You could try to use the "current second" block, but that will reset back to zero every time it gets to sixty. That won't work!

To do this, you'll need to use the "timer" block. It counts up from zero, starting when the project begins. When the script finally gets to the actual "timer" block, it will tell your sprite what that number is and run whatever block it's part of.

An easy way to see the timer at work is simply by having the sprite tell you how long it's been running for. You can add the "timer" block into the "say _____" block and then run it to see the timer in action. As soon as you click the green flag, your sprite will start showing how many seconds have passed.

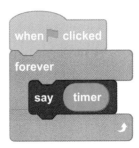

You might notice another block related to the timer: "reset timer." This starts the timer over at zero. You'll find this very handy if you use the timer when you make a game. Maybe you need to give the player some instructions so you don't start the game right away. Or maybe you want to reset the timer when you change to the next level. There are a lot of different reasons why you might want to reset the timer in the middle of the game.

Days Since 2000 Block

To more easily work out how many days before or after a specific date, you can use the "days since 2000" Reporter block. One way you might use this block is to create a list of appointments or events. First you would figure out how many days will have passed between January 1, 2000, and the day of your event. Then you can use some Operators blocks to show how many days between the two dates! Each time you start your project in the future, you will be able to see how many days until your event.

Asking Questions

Most of the Sensing blocks tell you very specific things. The "touching color _____?" block can only tell if your sprite is touching that specific color or not. The "timer" block tells you exactly how many seconds have passed when it runs. There's another block, the "ask _____ and wait" block, that can have any response the player wants!

When this block runs, it will ask a question on the stage and wait until the player gives it an answer and then presses *Enter* or *Return*. It doesn't matter what the answer is; the player can type a number, words, or even an empty response!

ALERT

Google "days since 2000 calculator" to find a handy date calculator to help you work out the number of days to your special date, such as a birthday!

Whatever the player decides, Scratch will make this the new "answer" variable. Now when you use the "answer" block, this is what will pop up!

Ask and Wait

Let's try an example. We'll keep it simple and just have your sprite say your name back to you. Let's add an Events block like the "when green flag clicked" block so we can get the project started. Next, add this fancy new "ask _____ and wait" block below it. Now we need a block to make your sprite tell us the answer. Let's go to the Looks category and grab a "say _____" block. Add the "answer" block to a "join" block so the Scratch cat can say "Hi" before the player's name. Then add that join block to the "say _____" block, and we're ready to go!

Other Sensors

We've covered most of the big Sensing blocks, but there are still a few more. Throughout the book, you've learned about ways for a sprite to find out where it is (using the "x position" and "y position" Motion blocks), what costume it's wearing (using the "costume _____" Looks block), how loud it is (using the "volume" Sound block), and a lot of other things. But what if you want the sprite to know where another sprite is, or what costume a different sprite is wearing? Then the "_____ of _____" Sensing block can peek across to other sprites or backdrops to find out even more things.

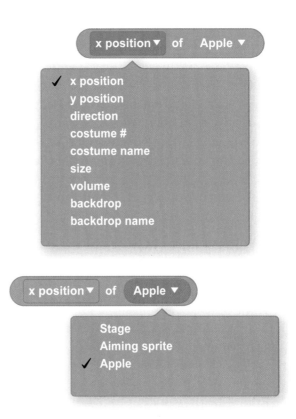

YOU CAN MAKE YOUR SPRITE REACT IN DIFFERENT WAYS DEPENDING ON HOW LOUD IT IS!

It might not be immediately obvious what the "loudness" block does. Does it tell you how loud a sprite is? Not exactly. In this case, the block connects to your microphone.

You can use this block to tell you the volume of a noisy room. You can make the sprite react in different ways depending on how loud it is! For example, you might set the size of your sprite to this in a loop like the following. This would make the sprite change from extremely tiny to its full size depending on what Scratch can hear from your microphone. You can literally see the sound!

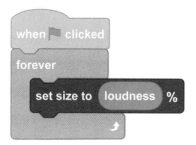

The very last Sensing block is the "username" block. This is a pretty simple one. This block will show the username that the person playing your project has logged in with. You can use this to personalize a message to someone playing your project, like with the following blocks:

Activity | Trobo Maze

MEDIUM

For this activity you will get to create a twist on a maze! When you go through a maze, usually it stays the same so you can work out how to get through it. But in this activity the maze changes while you go through it! Sounds crazy, right? Let's dive in and get started.

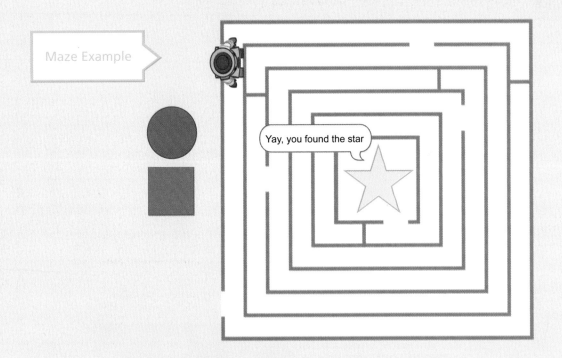

Maze Example

Yay, you found the star

1. Choose the Sprites

To start, you will need to create the sprites and the backdrops for the maze. This example is using a fun character called Trobo! He likes to tell stories and needs help to find his way through the maze. He's not a sprite you can find in Scratch, so choose whatever sprite you like best or draw your own and set its size to about 30 pixels by 30 pixels, the same size as Trobo is.

Now draw or choose another sprite. This will be the goal at the center of the maze. Now make four costumes for this shape. You can make them different colors and shapes, but you want them to be about the same size as the star, circle, and rectangle in the prior example, about 60 pixels by 60 pixels.

2. Create the Maze

Finally, create the maze. Be sure to go to the backdrops to create your maze since it is not a sprite. Your first idea might be to draw a maze with a bunch of lines and then add in some spots for the sprite to get through. You'll find, though, that this takes a long time. Since you're going to create four different maze backdrops, it's much easier if you start by using the Rectangle tool to just draw a few rectangles inside of each other for each layer of the maze. Do this in vector mode in the image editor (which you'll learn more about in Chapter 12) since it will be easier to change if you don't get it quite right. Make sure you leave some space on the left. You are going to use this later on.

Once you have all of the rectangles of the maze, add in a white rectangle to create paths through the maze. Do the same thing for all the gaps you want to make. To finish this off, draw some lines to block the player from going certain ways.

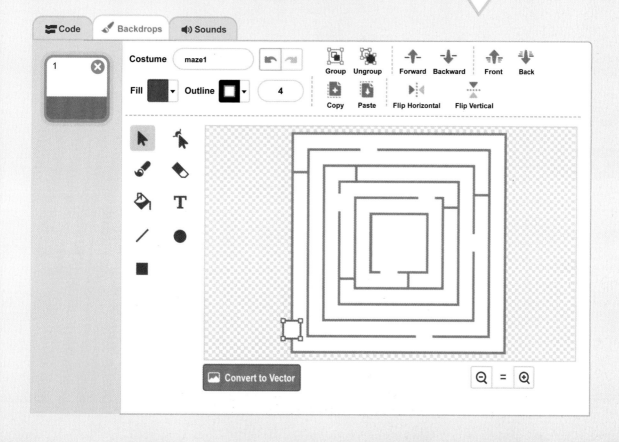

3. Create the Backdrops

Now right-click and duplicate this maze three times so you have four maze backdrops for your project. Change each of the mazes to have slightly different spots to get through and a few different blocking walls. Now you can get to the code!

You want the backdrop to change every thirty seconds for as long as the game is being played. How do you think you could make that happen? The best way is to connect a "wait 30 seconds" block to a "switch backdrop to next backdrop" block and then put both of those in a "forever" block. Just to make it a little more fun, you should add a chime sound every time the backdrop changes. How does your code look? It should look something like this.

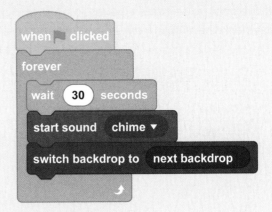

4. Move the Main Sprite

For the next step, you need to get your main sprite moving around. You always want to tell people how to play, so start off with a "say _____ for _____ seconds" block. Then you always want to bring the main sprite back to the starting point. If your starting point is on the left, you should have the sprite point toward the left so it can glide back to the starting position and then turn around to face the maze. The goal is to keep going until your main character is touching the target, so add in the "repeat until" block and add in the condition to go until it's touching the sprite you made ("touching target").

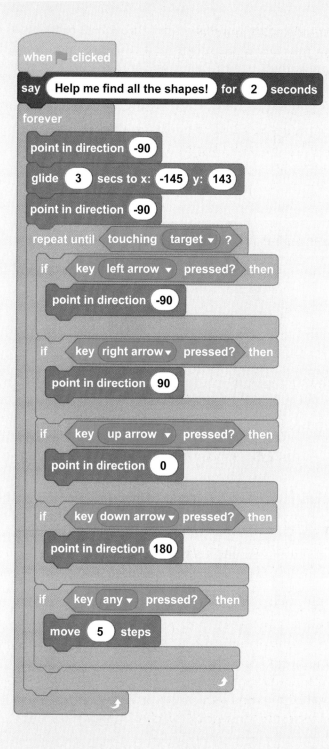

Next, add some Sensing blocks so the sprite will point and move in the direction of the key the player presses. It looks like a lot of code, but that's because you need to check for each direction key.

Now try it out.

Whoa, your sprite is walking right through all of the walls of the maze! You need to get him to stop if he runs into the wall!

To do this you'll need to add a sensor to the front of your main character. In this example, adding some white blocks in front of Trobo will help see where it's okay to go and where the maze is.

Sprite Sensor

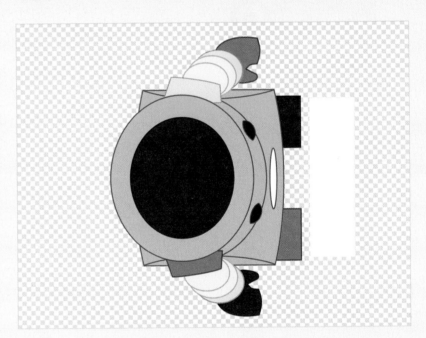

Now you should add the blocks to make it check if this white rectangle runs into the maze. Add a few more blocks between the "key any pressed?" block and the "move 5 steps" block to make it so it will sense the maze. The first step is to check if the white is touching the blue color of the maze. If it is, add a sound to make it sound like your sprite has run into the wall. Otherwise, your sprite gets to move!

Finally, add a "broadcast _____" block, and make "goal" the message. This broadcast will tell other sprites when your sprite has reached the target. You want to put it as the second to last block in the code since you want the message to broadcast only after the player has reached the target. Try it out again! Trobo should no longer go through the walls.

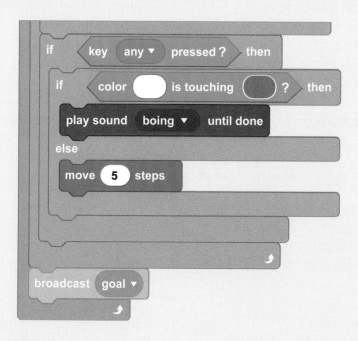

5. Add the Goal

Now it's the final stretch, the goal. First, you want the goal to change every five seconds so add a "forever" loop around a "wait 5 seconds" and a "next costume" block.

Now you need the goal to react if your sprite reaches the target. Remember that broadcast for the goal? When your sprite touches the goal, the goal should receive that message and check to make sure it's touching your main sprite. If it is, it should create a clone of itself so you have a little trophy!

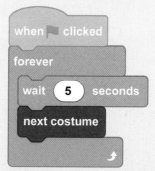

But you don't want the trophy in the middle of the maze. When the trophy is created as a clone, you want it to move off to the empty space on the side of the maze. When the goal starts as a clone, you should have it glide over to the left side (x: −210). You don't want all of the trophies on top of one another, so set the y position to space out each of the different goals. You can do this by multiplying the costume number by seventy (ten pixels more than the size of the goals you created—this will leave space in between the trophies on the side of the maze) and then subtracting that from two hundred. This will move each trophy down from the top of the stage (y: 200).

When you win, you should get to celebrate. To finish up this project, add a "say _____ for _____ seconds" block when the goal creates a clone. You could have it say something like "Yay, you found the costume name" of the goal you just got. Try it out! Your game is now ready to go!

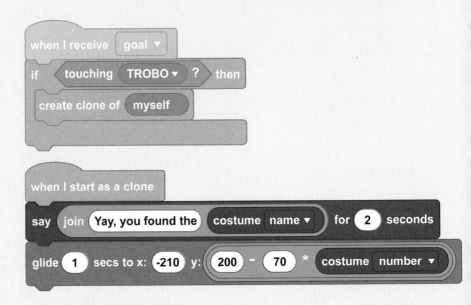

9

VERY VALUABLE VARIABLES

VARIABLES

You've already learned a little about variables, like the "switch costume to _____" Looks block or the "mouse x" Sensing block. Well, you can create your own variable too! Almost every project you make will need to keep track of things that change. Your projects have already been doing this for some variables (such as a sprite's location), but to take your projects to the next level, you'll need to be able to make your own variables to keep track of other important things for your project.

Variables

You might have heard about variables at school. Usually most schools teach variables as part of algebra courses in seventh or eighth grade. Don't worry if you have not covered it yet though. This section will teach you all you need to know!

Variables Explained

At the start of the year, you probably had to tell your teacher your name. Not everyone had the same name, right? A name is an example of a variable! The name of the person the teacher is talking to changes as the teacher talks to different people. One minute the teacher could be talking to someone named *Andrew*, and the next, he or she is talking to someone named *Brett*.

Name is your first example of a variable, and you see the different values it can have depending on whom you talk to. You do not actually use the word *name* when you meet someone though, unless you don't remember what that person's name is. You replace that variable with what that person's actual name is.

Variables don't just store words as their values. They can also remember numbers. For example, another variable in real life is your age. Your age goes up as you get older, so it's always changing!

Making Variables

To make a new variable, obviously you'd have to start in the *Variables* section! Choose the dark-orange *Variables* section of blocks, and you should see the *Make a Variable* button.

> **FACT**
>
> **Variable**
>
> A *variable* is used to represent something that can have different values. In Scratch, the value can be words or numbers.

> **ESSENTIAL**
>
> Variables don't always have only one value. For example, a variable like *score* can be used to show the current score in a game, and it can be changed whenever the game player does something good (or bad).

A NAME IS AN
EXAMPLE OF
A VARIABLE!

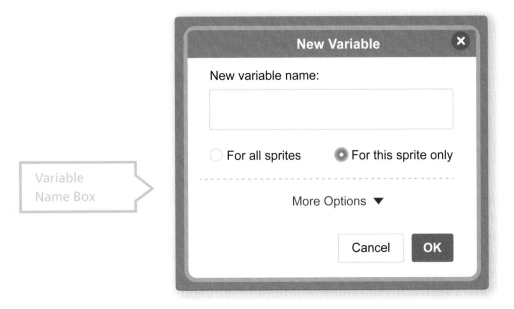

Variable
Name Box

Here you can name your variable. To make it easy to remember, choose a name that makes sense for what it's going to do. You don't want to make a variable and then forget what it does! If the variable is going to count something, like how many lives the player has left, give it a name like "Lives Left." Naming it exactly what you want it to do makes it easier when you have a more difficult project that may have many variables. Usually the variable name will never be shown to the person running your project, so it's more important that it makes sense to you than to others.

There are two more options to choose from when you create a new variable. You can select "For all sprites" or "For this sprite only," also known as *global* or *local* variables, respectively.

▶ GLOBAL VARIABLES

A global variable can be set or changed from the script of any sprite or the stage. It's global, and that means it is available everywhere. No matter what script you put a global variable in, you are always using the exact same one. You'll use global variables for parts of your project that are not specific to just one sprite.

FACT

Global Variable

A *global variable* is a variable that all sprites and the stage share in common. All sprites and the stage can get the variable or change it. If the variable changes, then it is changed so that it's the same for all other sprites and the stage as well.

A variable like *score* is an example of a global variable since there would be only one for the entire game. Different sprites can make the score go up or down, and all of them share the same *score* variable. The two examples of variables you read about earlier, *name* and *age*, aren't global variables. These are variables that are different for each sprite. These are examples of local variables.

▶LOCAL VARIABLES

If you select "For this sprite only" when you make a variable, it will be local. Can you think about things that are local to you, like your local school? Now think about a friend in another town. Your friend has his or her own local school, and it's different from yours. Your friend can't go to your school, and you can't go to your friend's school. This is how local variables work! Local variables are allowed to be used only by the sprite that it was created for. Other sprites will not be able to see or change a local variable.

Changing Variable Values

There are two ways to change the value of a variable. Just like you can set or change the *x* and *y* positions of a sprite, you can set a variable to a specific value or you can add or subtract from the current value.

The "set _____ to _____" block allows you to set a variable to something specific. You can use words or numbers here or even rounded blocks like the "timer" block. You'll use this block when you're first creating your variable so it has a value to change.

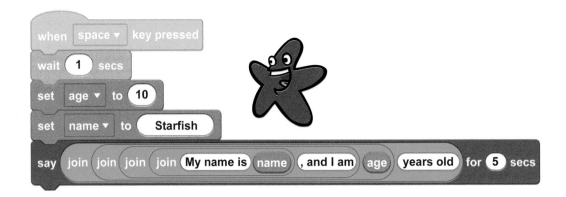

Let's take a look at an example to show you how to set a variable. When you press the space bar, the blocks set the variables for "age" and "name." This is done with the "set age to 8" block and the "set name to Crab" block. For the Starfish sprite, the blocks are the same because you are still using the same variables, but they are set to 10 and Starfish.

The "change _____ by _____" block allows you to add or subtract from whatever the current value for the variable is. This block works only if the value of your variable is a number. If you set a variable to a word and then try to use this block to change the value of the variable, the value changes to "NaN." What is this? This stands for *Not a Number*. It means you have tried to do math with a word! That's like asking someone, "What does 6 + pancakes equal?" It makes no sense, but it probably tastes great!

Showing Variables and Values

Just like with other rounded blocks, when you create a variable, you can show it on the stage. For example, you might want to show the "score" variable so the player knows how well he or she is doing. If you select the checkbox to the left of the variable in the blocks area, it will show up on the stage for the player to see!

Unlike other rounded blocks, there are a few different ways for the variable to show up on the stage. If you double-click on the variable on the stage, it will rotate through the different ways you can have the block appear. Each of these is called a *variable view*. There are three variable view options.

- Normal Readout: Score 0

- Large Readout: 0

- Slider: Score 0

The normal readout is the simplest. It will always show the name of the variable next to its value. This is great if you have more than one variable you want the player to see, like if each sprite has a different score.

The large readout shows only the current value of the variable, without the name next to it. This is the one you want if this is the only variable on the stage, like a global score variable.

The slider is a little different from the other two. It doesn't just show the value of the variable; it lets the player choose it! The player can drag the slider left or right to set the value himself or herself. You might use this to let the player choose how hard the game is or how fast the game goes.

If you right-click on the variable showing on the stage, a few options will show up. You'll see the three different variable views that you can choose between.

Display and Hide Variable Views

Just like you can show or hide sprites on the stage using blocks, you can also show or hide the variable on the stage using blocks. This can be helpful if you have different variables that you want to show at different times. Take a look at this script.

When "start level" (a made-up message for starting a level of a game) happens, this code hides the variables and then shows either the "bananas" or the "oranges" variables, depending on whether it's the first or second level.

Lists

A variable works when you want to remember just one number or sentence. But sometimes you might want to remember a lot of numbers and words, and it can quickly get really tough to do this with different variables. Instead of doing it that way, you can use a list! Think about a list you've seen, like a grocery list or school supply list. What if, instead of one list, each thing on the list were on a different piece of paper? Trying to keep track of that pile of paper would be annoying and make it really easy to lose one. Lists help keep things organized by keeping all the items of the same type in one place. Lists in Scratch can do the same thing for you.

> **FACT**
>
> **List**
>
> A *list* is a special variable that you can create to store multiple numbers or words together in one place. It is similar to real-world lists in most ways.

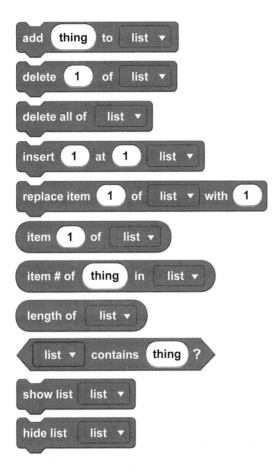

Creating a List

First you need to create a list. In the same dark-orange *Variables* section where you were making variables, you should see a button that says *Make a List*. You should get a pop-up box just like the one you saw when you made a variable. Go ahead and give your list a name, one that describes what's going to be in the list. Once you've created a list, you should see a bunch of new blocks appear. Don't worry; we'll go over what each of these do.

Once you have created a list, you can add items to it. In the following example, it will be a list of questions to ask. It doesn't have to be a list of words. It can also be punctuation, numbers, or a combination of numbers, words, and punctuation. You can change the content of your list in two ways. You can change it directly in the stage, or you can change it using blocks.

Changing a List Directly

The easiest way to change a list is from the stage! You can go right into the list and add, remove, or change the list as you'd like.

You should see a box pop up on the stage with your list name at the top, a little "+" symbol in the bottom left corner, and "length 0" in the middle of the bottom row. That plus symbol is what lets you add things to your list. Go ahead and click it! You can type in whatever you want to be on your list. Each item on your list is known as an *entry*. There's no limit to how many entries you can have on your list or how long each entry can be.

If you want to delete something from your list, first you need to click on the entry. You should see a little *x* at the end. If you click on that, the entry will go away. To change something in the list, you still have to click on the entry, but don't click on that little *x*. Instead, you can just delete or add whatever text you want.

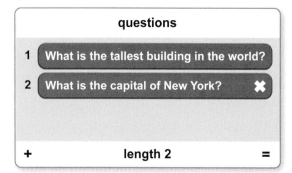

List Item
Delete Button

Add, Remove, and Replace List Items with Blocks

You can also change the entries with blocks. When using blocks to change a list, you use the list index. The *index* gives each entry a number to help you tell Scratch what you want to do with the list. For example, "What is the tallest building in the world?" has an index of one in the "questions" list and "What is the capital of New York?" has an index of two. You can always see the index of each item in a list to the left of the entries.

An index is also a variable, so it can refer to different items in the list. If you delete "What is the tallest building in the world?" from the "questions" list, "What is the capital of New York?" would move up. It would now have an index of one.

You need to understand indexes so you can use most of the list blocks. For example, the "delete _____ of _____" block deletes whatever entry is in the index number you put in. The "delete 2 of questions" block would delete "What is the capital of New York?"

The "add _____ to _____" block doesn't need an index number. It just adds the entry to the end of the list. Sometimes you don't care what order the entries are in. You just want all of the entries together on the list.

If you do care about the order, you can add an item into a certain spot on the list with the "insert _____ at _____ of _____" block. The first blank is for you to write whatever you want the entry to be, and the second is where you want it to go in the list, using the index number.

> **FACT**
>
> **Index**
>
> The *index* gives each entry a number to help you tell Scratch what you want to do with the list. For example, the first item in a list has an index of one. If a list has five items, then the last item in that list has an index of five.

> **ESSENTIAL**
>
> If you care what order the questions are in, then you will need to set the index to the correct place to add new questions.

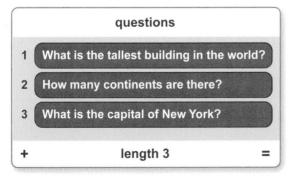

There's one last block for adding and removing entries from a list: the "replace item _____ of _____ with _____" block. This replaces whatever entry is in the index number of the first blank with whatever you put into the last blank. So "replace item <u>3</u> of <u>questions</u> with <u>How many states are in the US?</u>" would delete "What is the capital of New York?" and add "How many states are in the US?" at the same time.

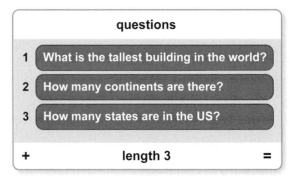

List Item
Replacement

Using a List

Lists wouldn't be very interesting if you couldn't get the items from the list when you need them. To use something from a list, you need to use the "item _____ of _____" block. This block doesn't do much on its own. It really needs to be combined with another block. It's shaped like a rounded block, so it can be used anywhere that has a space for that block shape. For example, since your list is all questions, it would be perfect to use the "ask _____ and wait" Sensing block.

In this example, a sprite asks one of the questions. You can also ask a random question by changing the index to be the random block from "1" to the length of the list.

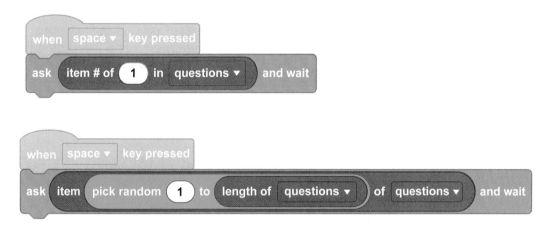

What if you want to ask every question from the list? How will you know how many questions to ask? Well, you can use the "length of _____" block inside of a "repeat _____" block. Then you have your sprite ask the first item on the index and wait, then move on to the next one, and so on.

Is It Already There?

Sometimes lists can get really long, and you can't remember if you already added something in. Instead of scrolling through the whole big list, you can use the "_____ contains _____?" block! If you want only one of the same thing in your list, you can use this script to check if something is already on it and then add it if it isn't.

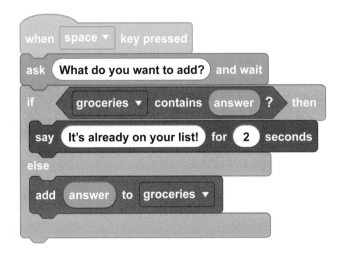

Parallel Lists

Many times it's helpful to have two lists that are related to each other. For example, you have a list of questions. You need answers, and you want them to match up with the right question! Let's add a second list of answers. Now you can write a code to ask each question and check if you got the answer correct or not.

Parellel Lists

questions		answers	
1	What is the tallest building in the world?	1	Khalifa
2	How many continents are there?	2	7
3	How many states are in the US?	3	50
+	length 3 =	+	length 3 =

Parallel lists might have more than two lists of information. For example, if you wanted your sprite to retrace its steps by creating lists of where it has been on the stage, you would need a list for the *x* position, a list for the *y* position, and a list for the direction of the sprite.

```
when [flag] clicked
set index to 1
repeat length of questions
    ask item index of questions and wait
    if answer = item index of answers then
        say That's it! You got it! for 2 seconds
    else
        say join No, sorry, it was: item index of answers for 2 seconds
    change index to 1
```

Remembering with Lists

You can use lists to remember the different values of a variable as it changes. If you want to remember the *x* and *y* position every time a sprite moves, you might have two lists for *x* and *y* to save the locations. The first part of the blocks here makes sure to remove all the items from the list so it doesn't continue to add locations from the previous times it ran.

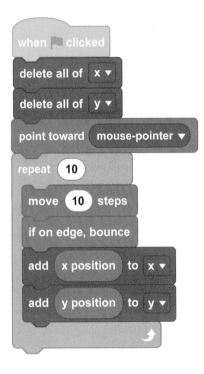

Now if you want to have another sprite do something else, you have a list of the previous locations of your sprite. For example, you could create a minion for your sprite that follows it to each new location after your sprite has left.

When you use a list to remember things for the current project, usually you will want to start out fresh each time. To do this, it's always important to erase the contents of the list when you start. That way it won't include any information from the last time someone played your project. If, however, you want your list to continue to add more things each time, then you can leave the items there so they will be remembered the next time.

Show and Hide Lists

Just like with variables, it's also possible to show and hide the lists on the stage using blocks. This way you can decide to show the list to someone playing your project just at the right time. For example, the list might only make sense to show to someone on a specific level. Or maybe you have a list of high scores that you want to show only at the introduction screen and then hide when the player starts. We can make that work with the "show list _____" and "hide list _____" blocks.

```
when 🏳 clicked
show list  high scores ▼
wait until < key  space ▼  pressed? >
hide list  high scores ▼
```

YOU COULD CREATE A MINION FOR YOUR SPRITE THAT FOLLOWS IT TO EACH NEW LOCATION AFTER YOUR SPRITE HAS LEFT.

Activity | Number Guessing

In this activity, you can create a number guessing game. The sprite will think of a number and then the player will have to guess what the number is. The sprite will give hints by telling the player if his or her guess is higher or lower than the actual number.

1. It's a Mystery—What's the Number?

Like all of the activities, your first step is to add your favorite sprite. You're going to want it to pick a random number between one and one hundred that the player will have to guess. That sounds like a job for the "pick random _____ to _____" block! You want your sprite to remember what number it picks, so you should turn that into a variable. Create a new variable and set it to pick a random number. For this example, you should call the variable "mystery number."

Now use the "ask _____ and wait" block to have the player enter a guess for the number. You will have two variables: the first one you created and the "answer," which will be the number the player types in.

You don't want to give a player just one chance to guess the number. That'd be impossible! Add the "repeat until _____" block around the "ask _____ and wait" block and make the condition check if the "answer" matches the mystery number. If it matches, the player has won! If it doesn't, it will ask the player to guess again.

ESSENTIAL

You can make a game get harder to play by using a variable to wait between doing things, like an enemy attacking. Start with a larger wait time between steps for enemies and then lower it as the game moves along so enemies attack more quickly!

If the player does need to guess again, you need to give the user a hint so he or she will know if the answer is higher or lower. After all, it's only fair to help the player out just a little. You could use a few "if/then" blocks to check if the answer is higher or lower than the mystery number. If it's higher, you could have your sprite say "Too High!" If it's lower than the mystery number, it could say "Too Low!"

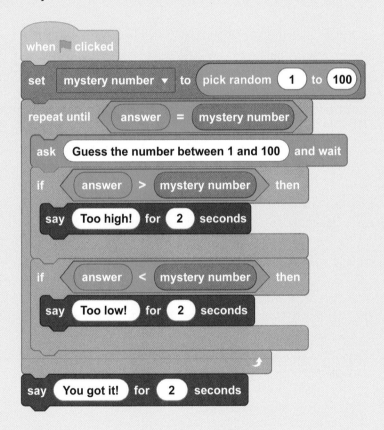

2. That Was FUN! Let's Play Again!

What if the player wants to play more than once? Well, you can make it so the game starts over pretty easily. To do that, you will have to repeat all of the blocks with a new question asking if the player wants to play again. Add another repeat block around everything except the Hat block to keep repeating the entire game.

But it needs a condition to tell it how many times it should repeat! You could ask if the player wants to play again. If the player doesn't want to, the game will end.

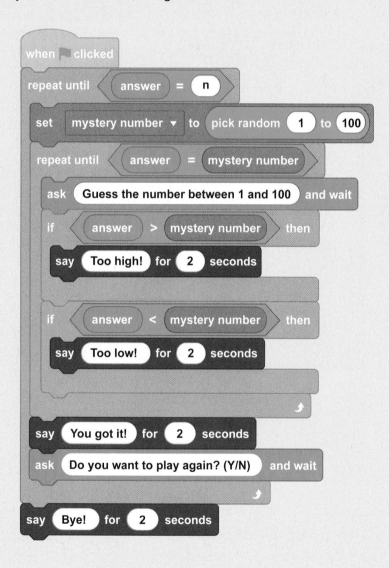

MINE, ALL MINE!

MY BLOCKS

As you work on more and more Scratch projects, you'll create some amazing things. But to make these amazing projects, you'll have to use an enormous amount of blocks as well. Every great programmer needs a way to keep work organized so that it doesn't become a big mess. Otherwise, it would be almost impossible to understand. Creating your own blocks can help you stay organized. But don't go too crazy with them! As any good programmer will tell you, knowing where and when to use them is an art of computer science!

Give Me Infinite Blocks!

Probably the best place to start learning about more blocks is by creating one. Let's start by going into the actual section of block. If you click *My Blocks* on the left, you will see a button called *Make a Block.* After you click on this, you will see a pop-up to create your new block.

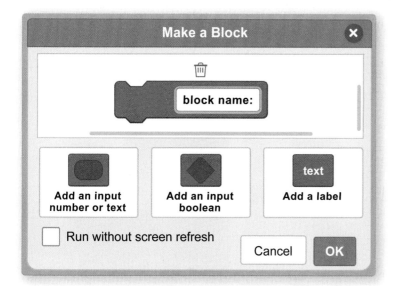

Make a Block Box

From here you can create a new block that can be used in the same way as other blocks you've learned about. There are three advanced options you can select here as well to add to a new block. For a simple block, though, you don't need to add any of these. Later, as you create more advanced blocks, you will see how to add spots to put oval or hexagonal blocks into new custom blocks.

For now, keep it simple and just make a normal block called "Dance." A "Dance" block should appear in your workspace that says "define Dance," and there should be a "Dance" block in your *My Blocks* section. However, the "Dance" block won't do anything until you tell it what it's supposed to do. So let's define "Dance"!

FOR A SIMPLE BLOCK, YOU DON'T NEED TO ADD ANY OF THE ADVANCED OPTIONS.

Under the "define Dance" block, let's add some blocks to make our sprite dance back and forth. We don't want our sprite accidentally going upside down, so let's add the "set rotation style left-right" block. We don't want this to go on forever, so let's add a "repeat until _____" block with a "timer > 2" operator inside. That will make it so this stops after two seconds. We should probably put a "reset timer" block before that as well, so we start over each time we want to dance. Finally, let's make the sprite dance. Add a "turn ↻ 180 degrees" block and a "wait .2 seconds" block. Now when you put the "Dance" block under an Events Hat block like "when this sprite clicked," it's ready to go!

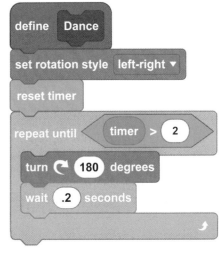

The best way to think about custom blocks is that all of the blocks of code connected to the "define Dance" block are inside the one "Dance" block that is under the "when this sprite clicked" block. So whenever you use the "Dance" block now, it just does all of these blocks. This lets you get your sprite doing these dance moves without having to copy all of the other blocks each time you want it to dance.

It is time to talk about a few names. When you create a new block, you are really creating something called a *function*. The function is the group of all the blocks, including your new "define" block. It's a good idea to try to use a name that makes it clear what the blocks are going to do so you don't forget later on.

FACT

Function

A *function* is a separate set of blocks that you put together that works on its own. In Scratch, functions are created from a custom block and start with the "define _____" block. You can use functions in a lot of different groups of codes without having to repeat all the blocks over again.

For example, using the name "reset" is okay, but "reset look" is better since it's clearer that the block is going to reset the look of only the sprite, but not anything else.

Inputs, sometimes also called *parameters*, let you add spots where you can add numbers, words, or other blocks into your custom block. All of the blank spots you've seen in the blocks, where you can change things, are inputs. The number inputs are the rounded spaces, like on the "move _____ steps" block. The Boolean inputs are the hexagonal spaces, like on the "wait until _____" block.

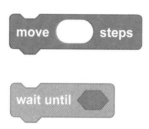

The values that you give to the inputs for the new block (such as the ten in "move <u>10</u> steps) are also known as *arguments.* These arguments are not like the ones you have with your friends or siblings though. This word just means *information.* So for our new block, the arguments give the extra information it needs.

Inputs are very useful when your script is getting really long. Say you want to add some different dance moves for your sprite. You could go ahead and just add all of the following blocks together to make some different dance moves. These blocks have the sprite doing three different dance moves for three different amounts of time. You might be able to guess what the different dance moves will look like by looking through each of the repeat loops and seeing how long each of them go for.

If, however, you want to choose which dance move your sprite does or for how long, it's not that easy to see exactly where to do this. Instead, you can use inputs to help you!

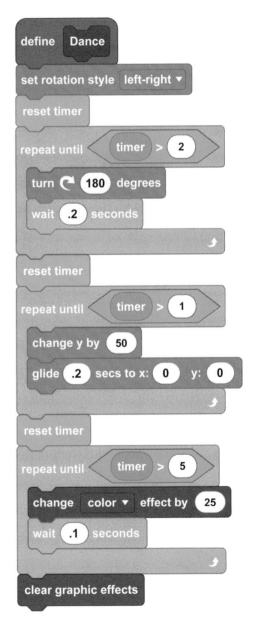

Try creating a "dance _____ for _____ seconds" block and adding a number input called "style," the label "for," another number input called "time," and the label "seconds." Then you can easily change which dance you want your sprite to do and for how much time. The script would look something like this.

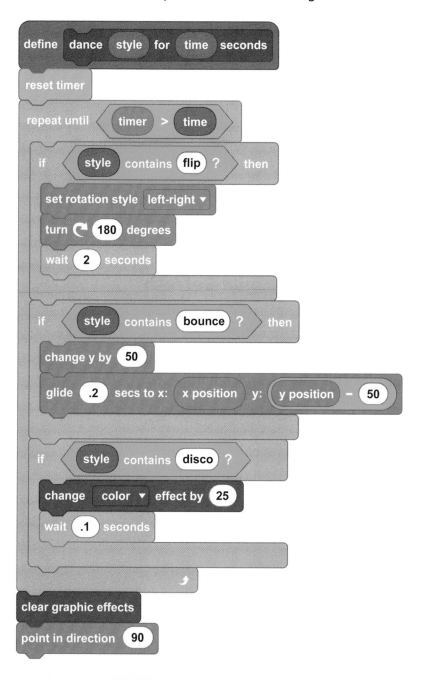

```
when [] clicked
dance (bounce) for (5) seconds
dance (flip) for (3) seconds
dance (disco) for (3) seconds
dance (bounce, disco) for (5) seconds
```

This does the same three dance moves as before, but now you can choose which dance to do, in which order, and for how long. The argument for the input can be "bounce," "flip," or "disco." By using the "_____ contains _____" Operators block you can even combine some of the dances together! With these changes, you can now easily rearrange the moves, repeat them, or change how long they will happen for.

Run Without Screen Refresh

There is one other setting you can make when creating your new custom block. That's the option to *Run without screen refresh*.

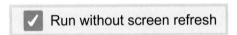

✓ Run without screen refresh

You can turn this on when you first create the block, or you can right-click on it and choose "Edit." The original pop-up you saw when you created the block will appear, and you can click on the *Run without screen refresh* checkbox.

SOME PEOPLE HAVE SEEN THEIR SPRITES GO UP TO 500 TIMES FASTER WITHOUT SCREEN REFRESH ON!

Let's see how this works. Let's create a new block called "custom glide" without the *Run without screen refresh* selected and add one oval input for the "steps" that it should make. Position your sprite in the bottom left corner and point it in the direction you want it to glide. Then have it wait one second so when you check *Run without screen refresh* later, you can see it move to this location, and then do the custom glide for 250 steps.

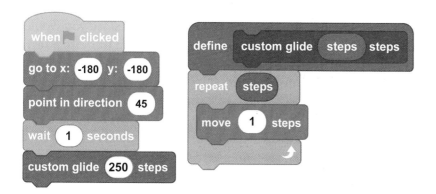

Now it's time to see it in action! Hit the space bar and watch your sprite move across the screen. Now right-click on the "custom glide" block, choose *Edit*, and then click on the *Run without screen refresh* box. Hit *OK* and then click the green flag for your sprite to take off!

Most likely you won't even see it take a single step from the beginning until it reaches its destination on the stage. What's happening is that, without screen refresh, Scratch doesn't show the sprite in its new location after each "move 1 step" block. It still does the actions, but they are so fast that you can't see them. It's only when the "custom glide _____ steps" block finishes that Scratch draws the sprite on the stage at its final location. This means that there is less work for the computer to do, and so it can go much faster than it otherwise would. That's why the sprite makes it from the starting point to the destination way faster. Some people have seen their sprites go up to 500 times faster without screen refresh on!

Recognizing When You Need Custom Blocks

Knowing how to make custom blocks isn't the only thing you need to learn. You should also make sure you know when to use them. The easiest place to use custom blocks is when you can see that some of your blocks all do the same thing. For example, a custom block that sends ten sprites to their starting locations and resets their size and color would make sense since you would only have to attach that one custom block instead of quite a few at the end of the code. It also helps you to clearly explain what a group of blocks is going to do when someone is remixing your project.

So far you've been dealing only with your own projects, but it's also possible in Scratch to work from projects created by others, which is called *remixing*. When you remix someone else's project, you are taking what that person created and changing it however you want. Some of the most popular users on Scratch have thousands of other people taking their projects and changing them. To become popular like this, these Scratchers take the time to make sure they use custom blocks to organize their code so that when someone like you looks inside their project, it's not so difficult to understand. If it's just one big set of blocks, it can almost be impossible to figure out what the blocks are doing.

So when you're making your code, ask yourself, "Do I already have something like this?" If the answer to that is *yes*, then it's usually a better idea to take the blocks you already have and turn them into a custom block.

Using custom blocks can keep you organized, let you use fewer blocks, help you understand what the blocks are doing, and make it easier to make changes to your project. Why not use custom blocks all the time?

Well, it's hard to know when the best time to use a custom block is. It takes practice and lots of trial and error. If you use them well, they can certainly do all these things. But if you don't name them correctly or make the code inside the blocks too confusing, your blocks might end up more confusing than if you had no custom blocks at all. The best way to learn is by doing, so get in there and start organizing your code!

FACT

Remix

A *remix* is what you create when you change someone else's project and make it your own.

Activity | Jump the Blocks

For this activity, you will create a game. A barrier will move across the screen, and Scratch Cat will need to jump over it. The more times it jumps over the barrier, the more points it will score!

1. Add Your Sprites

If you would like to, you can add a new sprite instead of Scratch Cat, but this example will be using it. Whatever sprite you use, move it to the bottom left of the screen. Now you need to draw your own sprite using the *Brush* icon. This is going to be simple. Just draw a rectangular block (make sure to select the *Rectangle* drawing tool) and name it "Barrier." You should draw this around 25 × 150 in size. You can see the size underneath the sprite icon on the left. This will be the obstacle that your sprite will need to jump over.

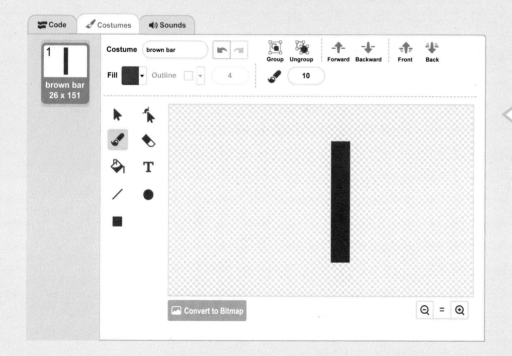

New Sprite in *Costumes* Tab

Now you should have two characters on the screen. Notice that in this example the Jurassic backdrop is being used, but you can use whatever one you want.

Placment of Two Sprites

2. Get the Cat Jumping

There are many different types of jumping that you can create in Scratch. For example, variables can help create more realistic jumping by adding gravity and speed to make it more like falling in the real world. But that can get really complicated. For this activity, you're going to create a simple jumping motion that just easily floats back down.

You've learned a lot in this book so far. How do you think you would go about making your sprite jump up when you press the space bar and then float back down? It might look something like this.

```
when space ▼ key pressed
switch costume to  costume2 ▼
change y by  200
glide  1  secs to x:  -170  y:  -130
switch costume to  costume1 ▼
```

Since Scratch Cat has a costume that makes it look like it's jumping, you can add in a costume change if you're using it.

Remember, it's always important to give instructions on what the player should do at the start of your game. It's also important to send your sprite back to its starting position with the "go to x: ———— y: ————" block. You should add those blocks in too.

```
when ⚑ clicked
go to x:  -170  y:  -130
say  Press space to jump the blocks  for  2  seconds
```

3. Move the Barrier

The toughest script to make in this project is the barrier moving across the screen while checking if it touches your sprite. So rather than using a lot of blocks in one long group, use the custom blocks to keep your code organized!

The first block you need to make is one to get the barrier to show up at the start of the game. You will also want a couple of variables to show how many times the cat jumps and how many times it successfully makes it over the barrier to move to the next level. Whenever the game first starts, you want those variables to be set to zero. You also don't want the barrier to show up while your sprite is giving instructions, so hide it at the beginning and then have it show up after the sprite is done talking.

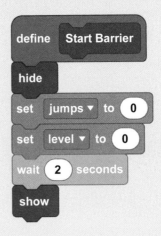

The next custom block will tell the barrier how to move. You need to tell the barrier where you want it to move, so start by telling it where you want it to start using the "go to x: _____ y: _____" block. But it isn't any fun if the barrier is always the same height or if you can guess where it will go each time! You can make it more interesting by having its height be random. Use a "pick random –50 to 50" block so you can control how tall the barrier is. Now each time the barrier sprite starts over, it will have a random height.

ALERT

Don't go too wild! You want your barrier to be the same general size.

Finally, you don't want it to move right away, so add in a "wait 1 seconds" block at the end.

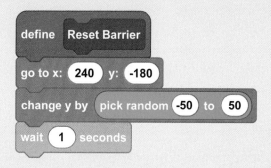

Now that the barrier is showing up when you start the game, it's time to make it move across the screen. Again, a great way to do this is to use some custom blocks. Create a new custom block called "glide barrier." You want the barrier to keep going until it gets all the way to the left side. You can do this by using a "repeat until _____" block where the condition is "x position < –235." That means this block will stop when the barrier reaches the left side.

You want the barrier to move horizontally across the stage. That sounds like a job for the "change x by _____" block! Just for fun, make the barrier move more slowly as the levels get higher.

ESSENTIAL

You might think you want the barrier to move faster as the level gets higher. It's actually harder when it moves slower because the cat could come down and land on the barrier. Then you'd lose the game!

Inside the oval input for the "change x by _____" block, you
can use an Operators block to make the barrier slow down based
on the level. If you multiply the level variable by two and then
subtract twenty from that, you'll get a negative number
(meaning the barrier will move left) that will get higher (meaning
the barrier will slow down) as the levels go up. As the barrier
moves across the stage, it should check to see if it's touching your
sprite. Let's create a custom block for that and then add it to the
"glide barrier" block.

Call this custom block "check touching." If the cat is touching
the barrier, the player has not successfully jumped over. The
player loses! To make this happen, use an "if _____ then" loop
and a Sensing block for when the barrier touches your sprite. You
will want to tell the player he or she has not been successful, so
add a Looks block to say "Try again!" when the barrier touches
your sprite. Once the player loses, the barrier doesn't need to be
there anymore and the game will end, so add a "hide" block and
a "stop <u>all</u>" block here too.

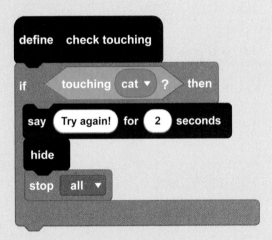

You have all of the custom blocks to make your barrier move
across the screen. Now you have to put them all together.

4. Put the Blocks Together

It only makes sense to start with the "Start Barrier" block, right? Then you want your barrier to go to the right spot, so the "Reset Barrier" block should be next. Finally, you should have the "glide barrier" block. You want the barrier to keep going back to its original spot and moving forward for the entire game, so you should add a "forever" block around the "Reset Barrier" and "glide barrier" blocks.

Now the barrier is moving across the screen, it has different heights, and it can tell if it touches your sprite. The last step is for your sprite to count how many jumps it has made. Then you can make it so the level goes up whenever the player jumps over the barrier five times. Start this custom block off by having the "jumps" variable go up by one each time this block is run. How do you think you can do this?

ALERT

Here's a hint: It involves a Control block and two Operators blocks.

To do this, you need an "if _____ then" loop and the "_____ mod _____" and "_____ = _____" Operators blocks. Remember that *mod* means the numbers left over when you divide the first number by the second number. So if the number of jumps is four and you divide by five, it will not equal zero. When "jumps" equals five and it is divided by five, the remainder will be zero and the level should go up! For fun you can also have the backdrop change each time a player is able to make it to the next level. Add your "check next level" block to the end of code that makes your sprite jump (the blocks that start with the "when space pressed" Hat block).

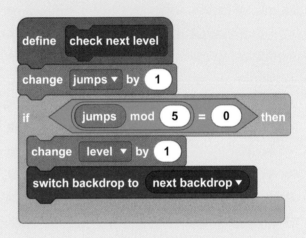

11

EXTENDING THE FUN

EXTENSIONS

Did you think you've seen all the blocks that you could use in Scratch? Well, there's more! In this chapter you will learn all about extensions, a bunch of fun blocks that can do a bunch of amazing things. But since you won't use these in every project, they are not available until you add them. This lets Scratch load a little bit faster for you. These extensions include music, speech, and video features, among others. There will be new blocks added here all the time so be sure to check the Extensions section often to see all the latest stuff.

In the bottom left corner of Scratch, you'll notice a blue button with some white blocks and a plus sign. If you click on that, you can get even more blocks! This *Add Extension* button takes you to the Extensions section.

Music

The first extension you'll see is *Music*. Using these blocks, you can play instruments and drums, even make your own songs!

There are a whole bunch of different instruments you can choose from. You might have heard of some, like the cello and saxophone, but there are also some really weird ones, like the vibraphone and the marimba. Try playing around with different instruments to hear what they sound like!

Music
Play instruments and drums.

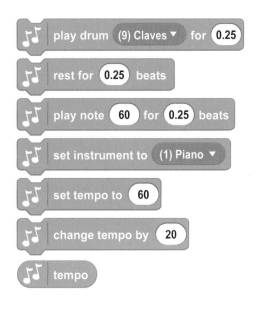

Music Extension Button

THERE ARE A WHOLE BUNCH OF DIFFERENT INSTRUMENTS YOU CAN CHOOSE FROM.

Playing Drums and Instruments

A really fun way to play these instruments is to connect the blocks to different keys on your keyboard. You can have the *a*, *b*, and *c* keys playing the drums and the *j*, *k*, and *l* keys playing some different instruments. You have your own orchestra!

If you press these keys really fast and in different orders, you can make some fun sounds. Add even more keys and different instruments to make it sound even cooler!

So what values can you put for the notes? Well, if you want to hear every note, you could create a "note" variable and put it in a "play note _____ for _____ beats" block. Add a "change note by 1" block and throw a "forever" loop around both blocks, and it will play every note in order for you. You will notice that the notes don't really sound like anything until the note value reaches about 20, and they stop increasing in pitch at about 120.

Rests

Have you ever gone to a concert at your school? Maybe you're in the band yourself! If you have ever been to one, you might have seen some of the band players sitting there doing nothing while other people are playing. They are taking a rest because there's no music for them to play during that time.

In Scratch you can create these breaks in the music by using the "rest for _____ beats" block. This tells whatever instrument you're using to pause for however many beats you choose. Usually one beat is the length of one note. This way, if you rest for one beat and everyone else plays one note, it will be the same amount of time and everyone will still be playing together. How long the beats and notes last for is controlled by something called the *tempo*.

Tempo

The tempo controls how long a beat is. The tempo is measured by the number of beats per minute (or bpm). So if you set the tempo to 60, then it will play one beat every second. If you want to speed up the music and get more notes in a minute, you can make the tempo higher. If you change the tempo to 120, then one beat will play every half second.

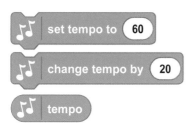

Let's see (or hear, in this case) this in action! Add a "set tempo to 60" block to any Events Hat block you choose. This block lets you choose what tempo you want. The tempo needs an instrument, so let's grab the "play drum _____ for _____ beats" block and put it in a "forever" loop so it keeps playing.

Now activate your script to hear the beat! Try changing the tempo higher and lower to see how the beat changes.

You'll also see a rounded "tempo" block. Just like with other rounded blocks, you can put this in any round input in another block. This can be useful if you want to have a sprite say the current tempo in a speech bubble or if you want to do something like change the tempo to half of what it normally would be.

▶ ADVANCED INSTRUMENTS USING TRACKS

When you listen to a band or concert, there are usually multiple instruments playing parts of the music at the same time. Each instrument that's playing is called a *track*. You can make tracks in Scratch too! This will help your music work together and really sound great!

Let's take a look at how we can make some music using tracks. Normally, if you put one instrument block after another, it will wait for the first one to stop playing before going to the next. You can fix that using the "broadcast _____" and "when I receive _____" Events blocks you learned about in Chapter 5. Since these send out their messages at the same time, you can have all of the instruments playing.

You want to play with three instruments, so let's use three broadcast messages, called "Track1," "Track2," and "Track3." You want these to keep playing forever, so let's add a "forever" block around them and add an Events Hat block to the top so we can start it. For this example, use the "when green flag clicked" Hat block. Finally, you want to give the instruments some time to play, so add a "rest for 1 beats" block after "broadcast Track3."

Now you want to make the band. For the first track, you need to start with the "when I receive Track1" block so it knows to wait for the message from "broadcast Track1." Then add an instrument, like the electric piano. It needs to know what note to play, so add a "play note 60 for 0.25 beats" block. But that will play only 0.25 beats! You want a whole beat! Add a "repeat 4" block around everything so it adds up to one beat.

Let's do the same thing with the second and third tracks. Add a bass drum for 1 beat under "when I receive Track2." Since it will play only 1 drum each beat, you don't need a "repeat" block around it. Now add a "rest for 0.25 beats" block under the "when I receive Track3" block and then choose an instrument. The clarinet sounds pretty, so you can use that. Add a "play note 65 for 0.25 beats" block to tell it what to play. That's going to play for only 0.5 beats right now, so add a "repeat 2" block to make it one whole beat. Your code should look a little something like this.

Press the green flag and listen to your music play. Great job! You'll be writing your own songs in no time! Try adding more instruments and changing the number of beats to make it your own.

when 🚩 clicked
forever
  broadcast Track1 ▾
  broadcast Track2 ▾
  broadcast Track3 ▾
  ♫ rest for (1) beats

when I receive Track1 ▾
repeat (4)
  ♫ set instrument to (2) Electric Piano ▾
  ♫ play note (60) for (0.25) beats

when I receive Track2 ▾
  ♫ play drum (2) Bass Drum for (1) beats

when I receive Track3 ▾
repeat (2)
  ♫ rest for (0.25) beats
  ♫ set instrument to (10) Clarinet ▾
  ♫ play note (65) for (0.25) beats

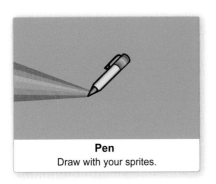

Pen
Draw with your sprites.

Pen Extension
Button

Pen

Now that you've become a master musician, you should learn to draw too! In the same Extensions section where you first saw *Music*, you should see a box labelled *Pen*. Click on that and you should get all of the Pen blocks to show up.

You can use any sprite to draw. The sprite is going to act like a hand on the pen. That means its location and direction are going to tell the pen where to draw. And just like the sprite can change its location and direction, the pen itself can change how wide it is, what color it is, and whether it is down or up. When the pen is down, that means it's drawing, like pressing a pen down to the paper in real life. When it's up, it's not drawing anything, like when you take the pen off the paper.

Using the Pen

When you use the pen in Scratch, you won't see an actual pen. Imagine the sprite is holding an invisible pen. It's going to do all of the actual drawing for you while you tell it where to go.

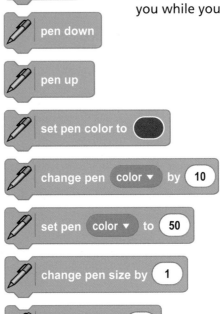

If you were drawing something in real life, you wouldn't choose just any old color or size for your pen. No, you'd want to choose just the right color and just the right width to make your drawing perfect. That's usually the best way to do it in Scratch as well. Choose your pen size and color, set your pen down, set the direction and location to move your sprite (remember it is holding on to your invisible pen), and let it draw the lines you need.

Before we get started with drawing things, you need to know about the "erase all" block. This block clears away anything that's already been drawn on the stage. It's usually a good idea to place this block after your Events starting block. That way you can have a fresh, clean stage to draw on. You might also want to connect it to a specific key using the "when _____ key pressed" Hat block so you can control when you erase your drawings.

Pen Size

You can choose the pen size using the "set pen size to _____" block and the "change pen size by _____" block. As the pen size gets higher and higher, the pen gets wider and wider. The nice thing about drawing in Scratch is that, unlike in the real world, if you want to change the size of the pen, you don't have to pick it up! You can just add the "change pen size by _____" block in the middle of the script, and it will just go right on drawing at a different size.

Let's see these blocks in action. Since you're just learning about drawing for the first time, let's keep it simple and just draw a line that changes how wide it is as it gets higher and higher.

The following example changes the pen width four times as the sprite moves up. Let's take a look at the code. You won't need to see a sprite for this to work, so you can hide it. First you need to erase everything on the stage to make sure it's clean. That means you should start with the "erase all" block. Next, you need to set the pen color (which you'll learn about in the next section) and the pen size, so grab a "set pen color to _____" block and a "set pen size to _____" block.

After that, you want to move the sprite, but you don't want to draw a line on the way there. Let's add a "pen up" block before we set the color to make sure no accidental lines are drawn, then move the sprite to the bottom of the screen and have it point up. Now that it's in the right spot, we can put the pen down so it draws the line we want. Now that everything's ready, let's have it move fifty steps and then make the pen wider by twenty. Repeat that four times and there you go! Your first drawing is complete!

ESSENTIAL

It might be hard to see, but the pen is round, not square. Take a look at the top of the line you drew. See how it's round at the top?

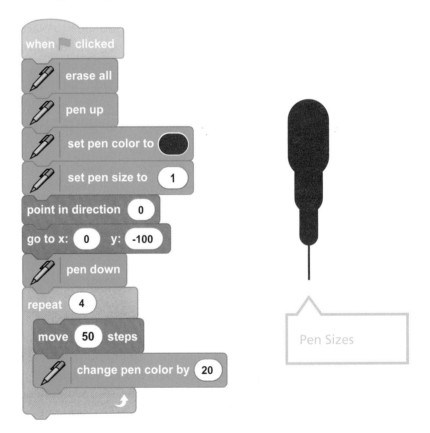

Pen Sizes

Pen Color

As you saw in the last example, you can also change the pen color. It is even better than in real life because you can change the color while you are drawing, just like with the size!

This example starts with a larger pen and changes colors twenty times while moving. Notice it has the same beginning blocks as the last example. This is to clear any old drawings and to make sure the pen is up as the sprite moves to the right spot.

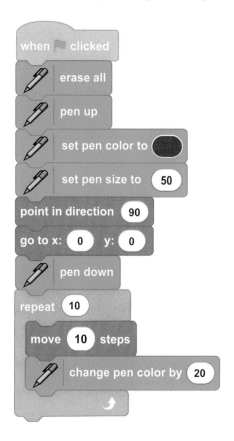

Pen Colors

You might notice there's another way to set your pen color, with the "set pen _____ to _____" block. There are actually a few different things you can set with this block. Besides the color, you can also set the saturation and brightness as well as the transparency.

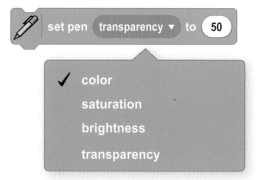

The transparency feature controls how much you can see through the color to anything else behind it. For example, here's a red line with its transparency set to 50. See how you can see some of the background but you can still see the red line?

Transparency

FACT

Transparency

Transparency measures how see-through the color is. At 50, it's 50 percent see-through, while 100 percent would be completely see-through and 0 percent would be completely solid and you couldn't see through it at all.

The transparency effect can be very useful when you want one thing on top of another but want to be able to see both. A great example of this might be adding a blue transparent drawing over a sprite of a diver. That makes it look like the diver is underwater!

Stamp

Have you played with stamps before? It's pretty fun to grab different patterns and stamp them on your page. In Scratch you get to do the same thing, but you can easily clean everything up with the "erase all" block!

Just like with real-life stamps, a stamp in Scratch is going to copy an exact version of what you want it to, in this case the sprite. If you've changed the sprite's effects in any way, the stamp of it will look like that too.

Here's an example of stamping a sprite and moving it across the screen. First it clears any graphic effects. Then it moves to the right, stamps the sprite, changes color, and repeats everything again. So why are there three? Well, one of these butterflies is not like the others. It's not a stamp; it's the actual sprite!

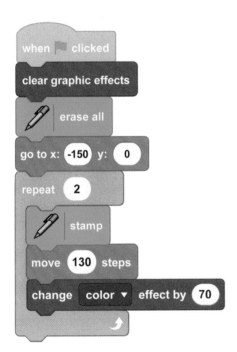

It's important to remember that stamps are not the same as clones. A stamp can't do anything. It's just a picture on the stage. A clone is able to run its own blocks and move around and do everything a regular sprite can.

Google Translate

The Google Translate extension allows you to change any text in your project to different languages. Whenever your sprite might say something, you can use the Google Translate extension to make it show up in the viewer's language automatically.

The input translates the same message into the language of the player playing your project. You can also ask the player what language he or she wants by creating a new "language" variable. Then use the "ask _____ and wait" block and have your "translate _____ to _____" block translate everything to that language.

Here the language is set at the start to the viewer's main language. Now when the player presses the *z* key, that player can switch the language to a different one. Try it out and see how to say things in all different languages!

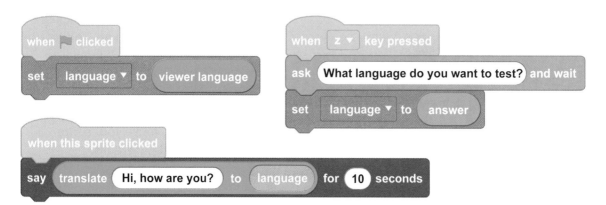

The "translate _____ to _____" block can translate to more than just the player's main language. It has many different languages to choose from. If you click on the drop-down menu, you can select any of the different language options.

Google Translate
Translate text into many languages.

Google Translate
Extension Button

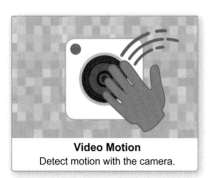

Video Motion
Detect motion with the camera.

Video Motion
Extension Button

Video Motion

If you have a webcam, you can use it to add video to the background of your stage. You can even use the camera to interact with your sprites! It's easiest to explain with an example. It's time to wave those hands!

In this example, three butterflies will be on the screen together with the live video from the webcam. The "video _____ on _____" Reporter block will tell you just how much motion from the camera is currently happening near your sprite and what direction that motion is happening in. You can use this sprite to do a lot of cool things, like move your sprite with your hand!

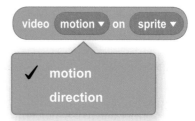

If you try out the following blocks, you will probably notice that the movement is really glitchy. You can use the "when video motion > _____" Hat block to help stop this. This block lets you decide to do something only once the amount of motion is over the amount you set in this block. This means it won't pick up any tiny little movements that you don't want Scratch to sense.

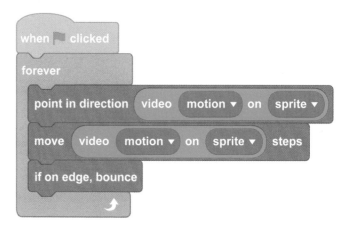

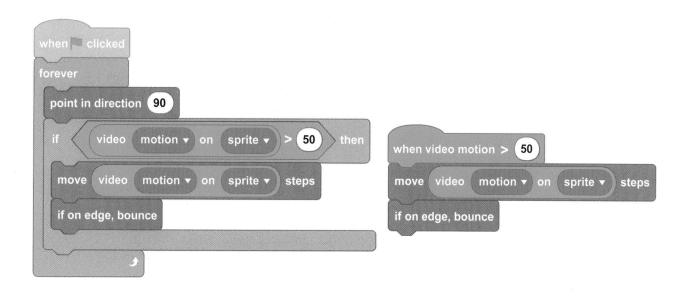

You can also do the same thing inside of a loop using a "_____ > _____" block and an "if/then" block. These work almost the same way, except that in the "forever" loop you will be able to continually do other things as well.

It's also possible to detect motion on the entire stage. You don't need to limit yourself to just a single sprite area. If you choose "stage" as the second input for the "video _____ on _____" block, you can decide to do something based on all of the motion that the camera can see, instead of just the part where the sprite is.

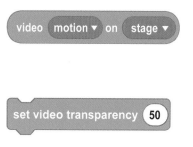

Sometimes you might like to see more or less of yourself on the video image. You can change how much of the video you can see with the "set video transparency to _____" block. This works the same way as the "set <u>ghost</u> effect by _____" Looks block does. If you set the transparency high, you'll see less of the video, and if you set it low, you'll see more.

If you want to control when the video actually shows up or not, you can also use the "turn video _____" block. This lets you switch the video on and off as well as flip the video so it's like looking in a mirror.

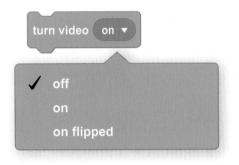

Have fun with the video blocks. Get your friends playing your games and waving their hands in the air like they just don't care!

Activity	Balloon Pop	★★★ HARD

1. Start Things Off Right

Just like with all the other games, you want to start this one by telling the player how to play the game. You also need to get some balloons set up, turn the video on, and ask the player how long he or she wants to play for. That sounds like a lot of blocks! You should probably create a custom block for this called "starting blocks."

If you are going to make balloons pop, then you can bet you'll need some balloons! Add a balloon sprite to your project and start programming its behavior. You want your first sprite to always start near the center of the stage so start your custom block with a "go to x: 0 y: –100" block. Next, you want the player to see how many balloons he or she has popped so create a "popped" variable. Have your "starting blocks" block always start with "popped" at zero and have it show up on the screen.

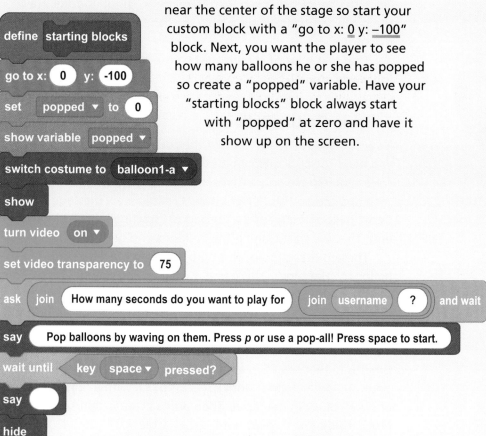

You also want the balloon to start on the same costume, so next you should add a "switch costume to _____" block. Make sure it always shows up with a "show" block.

Now it's time to add in a few of the new video blocks. In order for the script to sense any motion, video needs to be on. You don't want to see too much of the video in the background or else it might distract the player from the balloons. Add in a "set video transparency to 75" block.

Finally, we have to ask how long the player wants to play for and give some instructions. To make it more personal, use the player's "username" block in the "ask _____ and wait" block. Once this sprite has given the instructions, its job is done. Have the player press the space bar to start the game and then hide the sprite.

That was a lot of coding to start the project! How'd you do following along?

2. Bring On the Balloons

Now you should begin to build the code for the balloons. First you need to tell Scratch when the player is ready. Your main code should have only a "when green flag clicked" block and a "starting blocks" block right now. Create a new message titled "start balloons" and add a "broadcast start balloons" block to the end. This will start cloning the balloons and get them flying!

These blocks should start with a "when I receive start balloons" Hat block. This game is going to go on only for a specific amount of time, which means you'll need to use the timer. Add a "reset timer" block so there's a fresh timer each time the player starts the game.

Now you want the balloon to make clones of itself until the timer is higher than the answer the player gave at the beginning. You can add a "repeat until _____" block with a "timer > answer" block in the input. Then add a "create clone of myself" block inside the "repeat until _____" block.

Now create a new variable called "Time Left" to show the player how much time is left. Set that to be equal to the number of seconds the player said he or she wants to play for (the answer) minus how much time has passed (the timer). Don't forget to add a "show variable Time Left" block! It can also make the game more challenging! Add a "wait _____ seconds" block inside the "repeat until _____" block and have the input be "Time Left/answer." As the time runs out, the balloons will start appearing faster and faster!

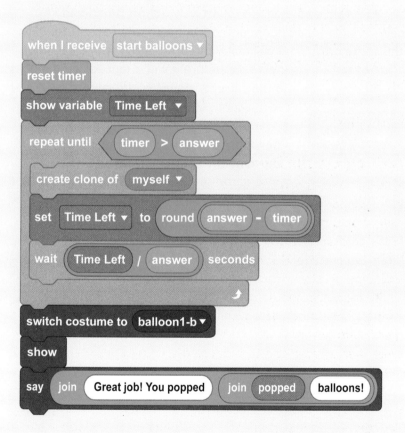

3. Pop the Balloons

Now you need to work out if the player has moved around enough over a balloon to make it pop. Since your balloons will all start as clones, you can use the "when I start as a clone" block to give them all instructions. You don't want all of the clones to appear in the same spot and always look the same, so start the code with a "go to random position" block and follow it up with a "switch costume to _____" block, a "set color effect to pick random 0 to 200" and a "show" block.

You want each balloon to last only a short time so add a new variable called "pop_time," but make sure to set it for "For this sprite only." This will make sure that each copy of a balloon keeps track of its own time before it will disappear by setting it to the current "timer" block value and adding two seconds to it.

Next you want to actually pop the balloons! You don't want any small movement to pop them so put a "video motion on sprite > 25" block in the input for an "if/then" block. Create a new block called "pop-it" and put it in the "if/then" block.

Before you define your "pop-it" block, finish this group by adding a "change y by 2" block under the "if/then" block and then finish everything with a "delete this clone" block.

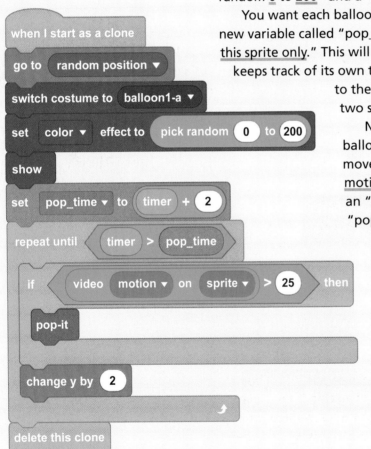

4. Pop It with Flair

Time to define that custom "pop-it" block. To make the balloon disappear a bit more excitingly, you can make it look like a balloon pops by making a new costume for it. Copy the blue balloon costume. In the image editor, switch to bitmap mode by clicking the blue *Convert to Bitmap* button toward the bottom left and zoom in a little bit. Using the *Select* tool (the one that looks like an arrow in a dotted box), select small areas around the outside of the balloon and drag them away from the center of the balloon to make it look like the balloon is popping.

Now define your "pop-it" block so it makes a popping noise and switches to this costume. You also want to make sure it increases the "popped" variable and waits a fraction of a second for it to pop before deleting the clone.

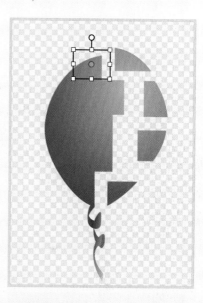

Select Tool

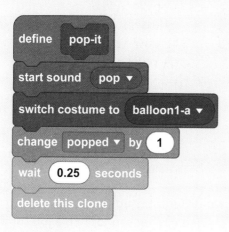

5. Enable Mega Pops

Now add in a mega pop. This will let the player pop all of the balloons shown on the stage. This will be triggered if the player presses the *p* key or makes a loud sound in the microphone. At the same time as starting the balloons, these blocks will also start and keep checking for the *p* key to be pressed or the loudness to become greater than fifty. If this happens, it decreases a new variable, "pop-all," by one and broadcasts a message to pop all of the balloons.

Start this group of blocks by creating a "pop-all" variable and setting it to five. This means the player can use this five times during the game. The player should also be able to see how many more times they can "pop-all," so remember to show the "pop-all" variable. You want the player to be able to do this until the "pop-all" variable reaches zero, so add a "repeat until _____" block and put a "<u>pop-all</u> = <u>0</u>" block in the input.

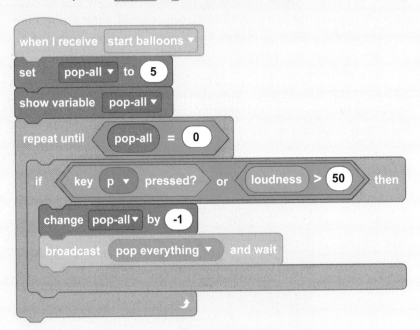

There are two different conditions you want to activate to use a "pop-all" variable. That sounds like a job for a "_____ or _____" block inside of an "if/then" block! You need to add a condition for when the *p* key is pressed or when the loudness is greater than fifty. If either of those happen, then the "pop-all" variable should go down by one and a message should be broadcasted to "pop everything." What does "pop everything" do? It's very simple: "pop-it"! This will pop every clone that is active at the time. See how many balloons you can pop!

ESSENTIAL

When you send a "broadcast" message and there are clones, each clone receives its own message for the broadcast separately and does its own thing. This can often be confusing if you don't expect it, so be careful using "broadcast" blocks when there are clones around.

THE PERFECT IMAGE

IMAGE EDITOR/IMPORTING

Scratch comes with some sprites and backdrops already built in, but to truly make a project your own, you need to create them for yourself. You can use some from your computer, take a picture with your camera, or even draw them yourself! The image editor in Scratch gives you all the tools you'll need to create the perfect sprites and backgrounds for your project.

The Image Editor Area

Before you can get started making anything, you need to understand what the different parts of the image editor are. There are three main parts: the *canvas*, which is the main drawing area; the *top toolbar*, which controls things like copying and pasting, flipping images, and undoing errors; and the *side toolbar*, which helps you draw and edit your sprite or backdrop.

The two toolbars can seem really confusing. There are a lot of different things to do with these toolbars. Luckily, you have this great book to help teach you all about what these toolbars can do! Remember way back in Chapter 1 where you learned about the differences between bitmap and vector images? Well, when you create images here, you'll see that the toolbars are different too since what you can do in vector mode is different to what you can do in bitmap mode.

The Top Toolbar for Vectors

The first thing you'll notice in the top toolbar is that this is where you can name the costumes. You can name it whatever you like, but just like with other things you can name in Scratch (such as variables and custom blocks), you want it to be easy to understand.

Right next to where you can name your costume, you'll see two curved arrows, one pointing to the left and one pointing to the right. These are the *undo* and *redo* buttons. If you accidentally make a mistake, you can quickly hit the *undo* button, which points to the left, and go back to how it was before! The *redo* button, which points to the right, basically lets you undo an undo. If you undo something and you decide you actually want it back, you can just hit the *redo* button, and there it is! Think of these like the *back* and *forward* buttons on your Internet browser.

> ### ALERT
>
> The first line of the top toolbar doesn't change when you select different controls from the side toolbar. It controls things you can always do with parts of the image. The second row of the top toolbar changes depending on which side toolbar control you select. You should learn about the top toolbar first. Then you'll learn about all the different tools and all of their options for the second row.

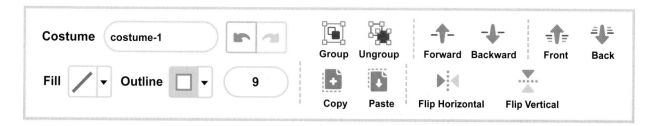

After that, you'll find the *Group* button for putting a few drawings into a group. To put things into a group, you first need to select more than one object. Click on the first thing you want in the group. Then hold down the *Shift* key and click on something else. You will notice that you can click on the *Group* button now.

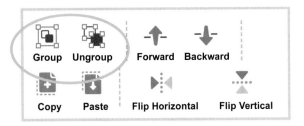

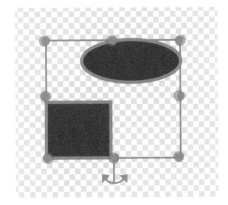

Once you group two things together, the things are now treated as one. If you click on one, they'll both be chosen. You can spin them, make them bigger or smaller, and move them around together without having to choose each one by itself. Once you've grouped at least two things together, the *Ungroup* button should show up. This takes two or more items that are grouped together and separates them again.

The next group of icons are for changing whether something is in front of or behind other things. Use the *Forward* and *Backward* buttons to move an object closer to the front or farther away. In this example, you'll see a pink rectangle in front of a purple square in front of a green oval.

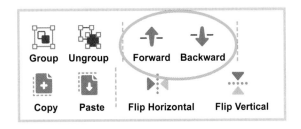

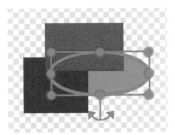

Each time you click *Forward*, the green circle moves in front of the next shape. So if you click *Forward* once, the green oval is now in front of the purple square but still behind the pink rectangle.

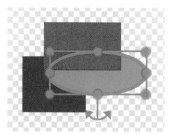

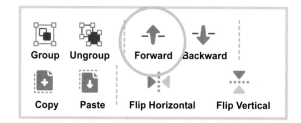

If you press *Forward* again, now it will be in front of both the pink rectangle and the purple square.

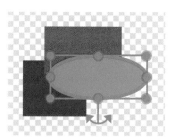

If you want something to go straight to the front or the back, you don't have to click *Forward* or *Backward* each time. If there were a lot of layers, that would take forever! Instead you can just click *Front* or *Back* to send it right to the very front or very back.

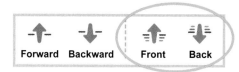

That's everything on the top row of the top toolbar. The second row of the top toolbar changes depending on which side toolbar item you choose. As you learn about the different side toolbar options, you'll also learn about the different things that appear here.

There are two other options, *Fill* and *Outline,* that you can change here. Depending on the shape you are drawing, you can change either one or both of these. For example, if you are drawing a rectangle, a different outline size will make the border much larger. Here is an example of an outline set to five and again set to fifty.

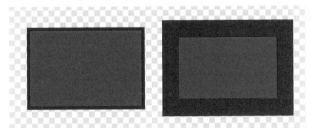

The Side Toolbar

The side toolbar has all of the different options for moving, coloring, drawing, or changing your picture in any way. There are nine different options: *Select, Reshape, Brush, Eraser, Line, Fill* (shaped like a paint bucket), *Circle, Rectangle,* and *Text.* As you can see, there are a lot of different things you can use to make your sprite or backdrop. Let's learn about what each one does!

The *Select* tool looks like a normal arrow cursor. It allows you to click and choose different things on your canvas. Once you choose something, you can move it, spin it, and change its size. Let's use an arrow sprite as an example to see what this tool can do. Once you select it, you can click and drag on any of the blue dots around its edge to change the arrow's size.

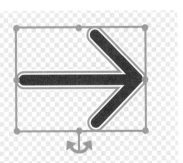

If you want to make the arrow bigger or smaller but you want it to look the same, hold down the *Shift* key while you're dragging the dots. Otherwise, you'll change the shape of the arrow like this.

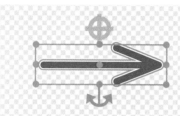

At the bottom of the box around the arrow, you'll see a little half-circle with arrows on the end. That's the *rotate* tool. If you click and drag the *rotate* tool, you'll change its direction.

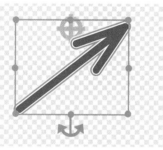

When you have the *Select* tool chosen, you'll notice that the *Copy*, *Paste*, *Flip Horizontal* and *Flip Vertical* icons are shown on the second row of the top toolbar. *Copy* and *Paste* do exactly what they do on the rest of your computer. They let you copy one of your sprites and then paste it back onto your canvas whenever you want. *Flip Horizontal* and *Flip Vertical* simply flip your sprites over. *Flip Horizontal* makes it turn the other way and *Flip Vertical* makes it turn upside down.

The *Reshape* tool lets you change the curves of any lines in your drawing or move the points around to change an image's shape. While the *Select* tool lets you choose points at the corner of the image to resize the image, the *Reshape* tool lets you move any point to change the shape of the image. For example, you could take the tip of the arrow sprite and pull it to the right.

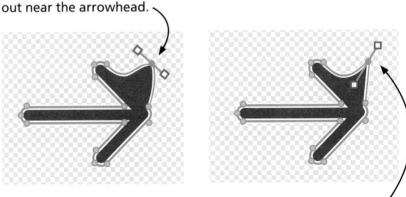

You don't even have to click on one of the circles on the line to reshape the sprite! If you click anywhere along a line between two points, it will create a new point so you can change its shape. In the following example another point was added and dragged out near the arrowhead.

When you add or select a point, a short line shows up. You can drag around the two ends to make the line change in some really cool ways. You can spin just that point around and stretch it in any direction! You can take that bulge you just made and curve it back toward the arrow to make it look really funny.

When the *Reshape* tool is selected, the second row of the top toolbar controls change to *Curved* and *Pointed*.

Curved Pointed

As you would expect, any changes you make to your sprite when *Curved* is chosen are going to look curved. Any changes you make when *Pointed* is selected are going to look pointy.

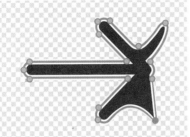

The *Brush* tool lets you draw whatever you want on the canvas. It doesn't have to be a straight line or even a line at all. You can make just a bunch of dots! Once you're done drawing, you can reshape and change the lines with the *Reshape* tool just like with any other image. The second row of the top toolbar will have only one option when you have the *Brush* tool selected. It lets you change the size of your brush, just like the "set pen size to _____" block.

The *Eraser* tool works just like the eraser at the end of a pencil. It's for those times you need to wipe something out. Maybe it's something a little extra you don't need or some drawing that went a little crazy. The *Eraser* will wipe it away for you. For example, let's say you didn't like all of the crazy changes to the arrow. You can just erase that entire half!

ESSENTIAL

If you need to erase a lot of something, it's helpful to start with a large size to take out a lot of it and then change to a smaller size. Zoom in so you can find all of the smaller mistakes you want to erase.

The option on the second row of the top toolbar for the *Eraser* tool is the same as for the *Brush*. It lets you change the size of the *Eraser*, from one to four hundred, depending on how much you want to erase at once.

Outline ▢ ▾ (5)

The *Line* tool does exactly what you think. It draws a straight line between two points! If you want the line to go only left/right, up/down, or diagonal, you can hold *Shift* and draw a perfect horizontal, vertical, or diagonal line. The second row of the top toolbar option for the *Line* tool allows you to change the width of the line.

The *Fill* tool (looks like a paint bucket) changes the entire color of the image. For example, if you use the *Fill* tool on the arrow while the *Fill* is purple, it will look like this.

You can change the *Fill* color from the second row of the top toolbar when using the *Fill* tool.

The *Circle* tool draws circles or ovals. If you hold *Shift*, this tool will make sure your drawing is perfectly round. The options on the second row of the top toolbar allow you to change how wide the outline of the circle or oval is as well as its color. If you don't want an outline, click on the red diagonal line in the bottom left corner of the *Outline* box.

Just like the *Circle* tool lets you draw circles and ovals, the *Rectangle* tool can draw rectangles and squares. If you are holding the *Shift* key, it will draw perfect squares for you. The options also let you change the border color and width, as well as the *Fill* color.

T The *Text* tool lets you type whatever you want as part of a sprite. You can choose the color of the text and the font for your text (even Chinese, Japanese, or Korean fonts) from the top toolbar. Click on the editing area to choose where you want to put some text and then just start typing!

Those are all of the tools for when you're editing vector sprites. If you switch to bitmap, most of the tools are the same but a couple are just a little different.

Bitmap Sidebar Tool

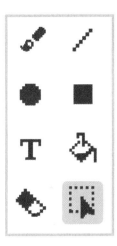

The controls are very similar to the vector ones, but once you switch to the bitmap tools, the sidebar basically groups everything together and doesn't let you ungroup them. You can't select the shapes you draw or change them around as easily as you can with the vector tool, so be very careful before you switch.

The first seven of these tools are more or less the same as the ones in vector mode. They do the same things as the *Brush*, *Line*, *Circle*, *Rectangle*, *Text*, *Fill*, and *Eraser*. The last tool on the toolbar, *Select*, works differently for bitmap mode though.

The *Select* tool in bitmap mode lets you choose some or all of the image. Then you can change the size of just that section, spin it around, or move it wherever you want it to go. Unlike in vector mode, where you have to select all of the image, you can take only a piece of it. For example, you can take just half of Scratch Cat and enlarge it.

The *Select* tool also lets you copy parts of an image using *Copy* and *Paste* mentioned before. Choose this tool and then draw a square around the part of the image you want to copy. Then you can drag this copied area wherever you want and change it around. Maybe you have a rocket ship and want it to have another fin. You can select and duplicate it, then rotate it to fit on the side!

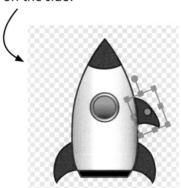 

You've got to balance the ship so do it again for the other side. This will probably get a bit closer to breaking light speed!

The last set of controls are at the bottom right below the canvas. They let you zoom out, reset the zoom, and zoom in. Zooming in is really useful when you want to change just a few small things. It makes it a lot easier to see exactly what you want to change. Once you're done, you can zoom back out so you can see your whole sprite again.

ZOOMING IN IS
REALLY USEFUL WHEN YOU
WANT TO CHANGE JUST
A FEW SMALL THINGS.

I Can See Right Through You!

Did you notice that the image editor has a weird checkered background pattern? What is this about? It means there's nothing there. Even white is a color, and it will cover up other sprites. For example, look at these three filled-in shapes. One of them is white, but it still covers up the purple square and a bit of the green circle.

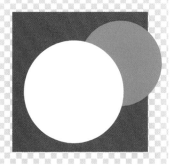

If you put this on top of Scratch Cat, you'll see that the checkered areas are see-through but the white circle is not.

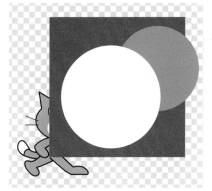

This difference between white pixels (or any other color) and the checkered background is important when you want sprites to move together. If there is a white background, it might accidentally cover up the other sprite. Scratch uses a red diagonal line to show this special transparent color.

Activity | Meteor Shower

HARD

This is the last activity in the book, so let's see what you've learned! In this activity you'll get to create a side-scroller game to help a rocket dodge a meteor shower. A good example of a side-scroller game would be one of the original Mario games, where Mario runs across the screen grabbing coins and squashing mushrooms. Side-scroller games scroll the background back and forth to make it look like the player is moving through a much larger space than the area of the screen.

This is what the final game is going to look like. This activity uses some drawing techniques to make your own sprite as well as an extra costume to make it look like you're rocketing through space!

Moon Backdrop

You're also going to use a lot of custom blocks. This is a complicated game to create, so it's really important to keep your code organized. Easy-to-understand custom blocks are a must!

1. Create Your Rocket and Your Background

The first thing you need to do is make a rocket. Go to the Internet and find a picture of one. You just learned how to take off the background and make it your own in this chapter. Make sure you clear away any pixels in the background and to make them transparent and not white.

2. Get Ready on the Launchpad

There are a few things you'll need to do to start the game. First, you want the rocket to start near the middle of the screen at the start of every game, so add a "go to x: 0 y: –16" block to the rocket sprite. Then we're going to create three variables: "worldx," "Score," and "Lives." You've seen the score variable earlier in the book, and you've probably played a video game where you have only a certain number of lives. You're going to want to show both of those variables so the player can follow along.

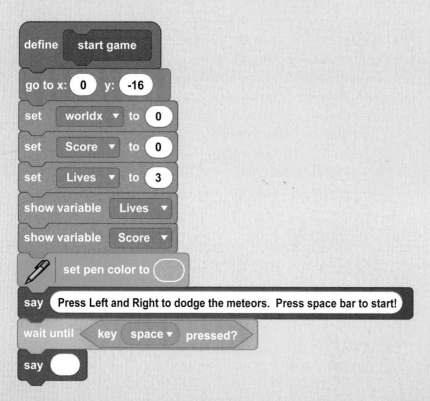

ALERT

You should use a background that looks like you're in space. You can find that on the Internet too and upload that as your backdrop or choose one from the backdrop library such as the Moon, Stars, or Galaxy.

The "worldx" is a new variable. The game is going to go farther than the edge of the screen, so this variable is going to keep track of which part of the world the game is currently looking at.

You need to give the player some instructions or they won't know what to do! Add a "say _____" block and add "Press Left and Right to dodge the meteors. Press space bar to start!"

3. Blast Off!

Just like a lot of other games, you will need a main game loop. It's common in many games to have one loop that does all of the main work of the game. This loops over and over until the game ends. The main game loop is usually responsible for moving things based on the player hitting keys, checking if collisions between sprites have happened, and updating anything that is falling or moving as well. By doing this all in one loop it's easier to keep things in order.

We just created the block to start the game. That happens just once at the start. Then this loop will check if the ship is moving. If it is, it will make a little rocket flame appear. Then it will move the ship to the left or the right. Finally, it will draw the left and right borders if it needs to. The short wait at the end helps other sprites animate a little more smoothly by not trying to run all the time. Since you want all of this to keep going until the player is out of lives, add a "repeat until _____" block with a "Lives = 0" Operators block in the input.

4. Do Move Flame

Let's start by adding a simple special effect to the rocket ship: flames! To get this working make a copy of the rocket's costume and edit the second costume to have no flames. If your rocket doesn't start with flames, use the image editor to draw some flames at the bottom and put them behind your rocket.

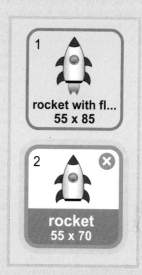

Now you just need to add some code to the rocket that checks if the *left* or *right arrow* keys are pressed. The following blocks check to see if the *left* or *right arrow* keys are not pressed. Why? Well, every time a player stops pressing the *left* or *right arrow* keys, you need the rocket to point back up. This will do that for you. When the *left* or *right arrow* keys are pressed, it will go through the cycle of costumes (with and without a flame) because of the "next costume" block.

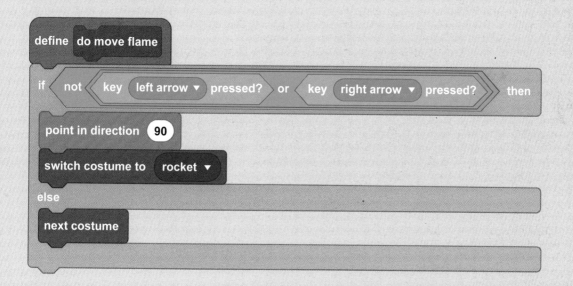

5. Move Ship

Now let's figure out how to make the ship actually move left and right. The first thing to understand is that the custom "move ship" block isn't actually going to make the ship move! Say what? Yes, in this game, the ship will always stay in the center and just look like it's moving left and right. The background is what's actually going to move. This is where the "worldx" variable comes in. You'll see where to use this variable when you add the meteors in. The "worldx" variable will control which part of the larger world the rocket ship is in. The rocket ship can scroll to the left or the right by increasing or decreasing the value of "worldx" since you will add this to the location of all the sprites.

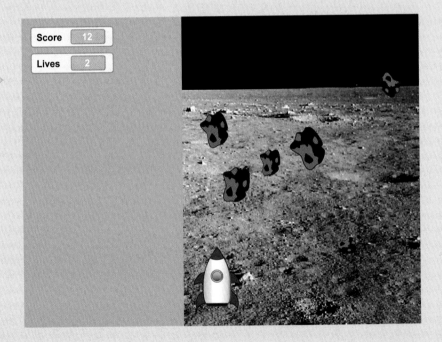

Stage Limit

As you go left across the stage, the variable value is going to increase, and as you go right, it's going to decrease. There needs to be a limit for how far it can go or else we're going to go right off the screen!

Let's start with two "if/then" blocks since you have two different things you want to check for. First, let's make it so you tell your rocket what to do when you press the *left arrow* key. You want to check two things here too. You can't be off the stage, and you have to press *the left arrow* key. That means you should probably use a "_____ and _____" block.

In the first input for the "_____ and _____" block, you want to make sure you're still on the stage. Add a "worldx < 200" Operators block there. Next you want to make sure the *left arrow* key is being pressed. There's a Sensing block that can do just that. Add the "key left arrow pressed?" block in the second input.

Now that the "if/then" knows what it's looking for, let's tell it what to do when it senses that. If you are pressing the *left arrow* key, you probably want it to go left. So add the Variables block "change worldx by 5." A "point in direction 60" block adds some extra effect. It will rotate the ship left and right to match the direction of movement. Now do the same thing for *the right arrow* key. Remember, since you're going in the opposite direction, everything should be the opposite. When you're done, your script should look something like this.

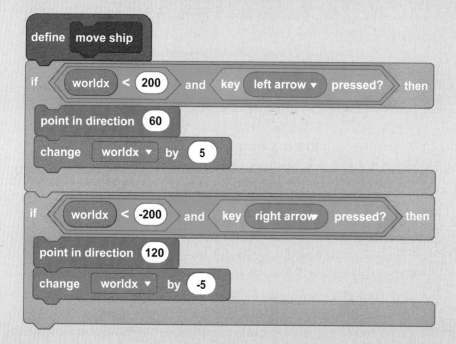

6. Draw Borders

To show a player where the edge of the world is, you need to draw borders. Do this using Pen blocks. You want it to happen instantly so turn off screen refresh for this custom block. These blocks will draw a border on the left or right, depending on the "worldx" variable.

You are going to make use of the ship sprite to draw the borders for you. This will make sure you draw the border at the right time, after the ship moves to the left or right. The first thing you want to do is make sure the player doesn't see the ship when it moves around to draw the border. Let's start with a "set size to 0%" block. That way the ship will disappear when it draws the border. Because it runs so fast, no one will even notice it's gone. We want to make sure we start off with a clean screen each time, so add the "erase all" block.

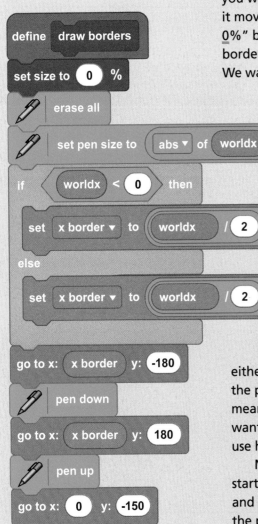

Now we need to draw the actual lines that will be our border. We want the line to get wider as we go farther left or right. By setting the pen size to "abs of worldx" it will do just that! Remember, "abs" (or the absolute value) changes all negative numbers into positive numbers. So once we go over to the right side, "worldx" will become negative and keep getting smaller, but the absolute value will stay positive and get bigger!

Then you need to put the center of the pen (or the ship sprite) in the middle of the border area by dividing the "worldx" by two and shifting it to the correct side. You are going to draw a border that is the width of "worldx" from either the left side (–240) or the right side (240). But in Scratch, the pen draws everything to both the left and right side. That means you need to position the pen halfway across the area you want to draw and put it in the middle, which is why you need to use half of the "worldx" value here.

Now all that's left is to actually draw it. You want the line to start at the very bottom of the screen (y: –180), put the pen down, and draw all the way up to the very top (y: 180) before it picks up the pen. Then you want it to go back to where it was before, so add a "go to x: 0 y: –150" block so it centers itself at the bottom of the screen. Hey, presto, a big gray border is drawn!

Now you have all of your blocks made for your rocket ship. That was a lot of coding. Nice work! Now you're ready for some meteors!

7. It's Raining Meteors

Just like you found a fun sprite for your rocket ship, go ahead and find a fun image that you'd like your ship to dodge. Since you're in outer space, a meteor would make sense. Remember to change its size to be close to that of the rocket sprite!

Meteor Example

Now you just need to get the meteor falling! You want it to start at the same time as the game, so you should use the same "when green flag clicked" Hat block that you used with the rocket ship. You want it to start off hidden and at the top of the stage. It has to also wait for the space bar to be pressed since this starts the game. Otherwise the rocket ship would have to dodge it before it could move, and that's not fair!

You want meteors to be falling for the entire game, so you need a "forever" block, and you want a little bit of time between each one. Add a "wait _____ seconds" block inside of the "forever" block. For that input, let's add a "pick random 1.0 to 1.5" Operators block to make it a little trickier for the player to guess when the meteors are going to fall. Now we just need a way to make a lot more meteors appear all over the screen.

We can do that with a custom block. Let's name it something like "clone meteor." Cloning the meteor is pretty straightforward. By turning the meteor each time, each meteor will look slightly different when falling, so let's start with a "turn ↻ 15 degrees" block.

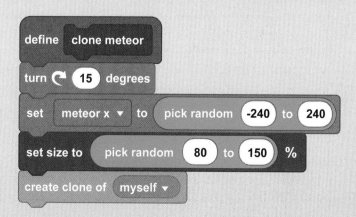

Then you need to set its *x* location somewhere random between −240 and 240 with a new variable. Because this uses "worldx," you need to put the *x* location into a new variable. Since the *x* location of the meteor will shift left and right as the "worldx" position changes, the meteor needs to remember its place in the world. Finally, you should make it a little more challenging by adding some blocks that are a little bit bigger and some that are a little bit smaller. You can do that with a "set size to _____%" block with a "pick random 80 to 150" block inside. Finish the script for the "clone meteor" block by having it create a clone of itself.

Now that we have the code for the "clone meteor" block, let's add it into our script. We want it to clone itself as long as the game is going on, so let's place it right below the "wait pick random 1.0 to 1.5 seconds" block. Your script should look like this.

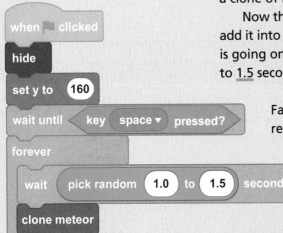

Once the new clone is created, it needs to fall. Falling starts by showing the sprite. Then you want it to repeatedly move down until it either touches the rocket or reaches the bottom of the stage. That means you want a "repeat until _____" block. Since there are two things that could stop this block, you need a "_____ or _____" block with the two conditions in there. If the meteor reaches the bottom of the stage, its *y* position will be less than −150, so you should add a "y position < −150" block in the first input. The second way you can end it is if it touches the rocket. For that, a simple "touching rocket" Sensing block should work.

Each movement of the meteor will first set its *x* location to its overall position in the world. This way it will go off the screen to the left and right when the ship scrolls in either direction. The meteor will get a little spin to make it more interesting, and each move will change its *y* value by −4 to move it toward the bottom of the screen. If the meteor goes off the stage to the left or right, when it is less than or greater than −239 or 239, hide it altogether so there isn't a tiny little bit of the asteroid sprite still visible on the side of the stage.

```
when I start as a clone
show
repeat until  < y position < -150 > or < touching rocket ▼ ? >
    move asteroid
    wait 0.01 seconds
    if < Lives = 0 > then
        delete this clone
increase score or lose life
delete this clone
```

```
define move asteroid
set x to ( worldx - meteorx )
turn ↻ 5 degrees
change y by -4
if < x position < -239 > or < x position > 239 > then
    hide
else
    hide
```

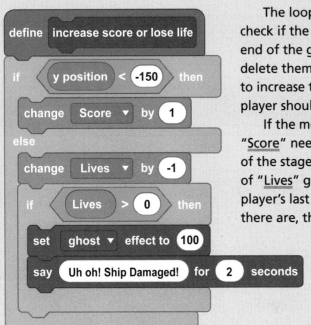

The loop here moves the asteroid each time but also has to check if the player has run out of lives. That would mean the end of the game, so all of the clones would need to stop and delete themselves. When the loop finishes, you need to check to increase the score (if the meteor hit the bottom) or if the player should lose a life (if the meteor hit the rocket ship).

If the meteor reaches the bottom of the stage, then the "Score" needs to go up by one. If it doesn't reach the bottom of the stage, that means it hit the rocket ship and the number of "Lives" goes down by one. To make sure that wasn't the player's last life, the script checks if there are any lives left. If there are, the ship is only damaged, not destroyed. Use "set ghost effect to 100" to hide the meteor (since if you "hide" the sprite, it will not show its speech bubble) and have it say "Uh oh! Ship Damaged!" Luckily for the player, there is still another chance!

8. Challenge Options

There are a couple of ways you can make the game even tougher. First, try making the world a little wider. This gives the ship more space to move, but there is also more space for meteors to fall! You will need to modify some of the places that don't include "worldx" (like the locations that specifically use 240 or –240 for the edge values).

Add levels and speed up how fast the meteors fall. Or maybe make them larger so it's harder for the player to dodge. Add extra costumes for your meteors and switch them up for special "power-up" meteors that, instead of doing damage, add health or lives!

INDEX